PRAISE FO

Regardless of where you are in your journey, the empowering stories and strategies shared in *She Leads* will guide you to lead unapologetically with grace and authenticity. You have a seat at the table, and this book will ignite a fire in you to claim it. If you are ready to be inspired to make the necessary moves now and evolve with the long view in mind, this book is a must-read!

—**Lainie Rowell,** lead author of *Evolving Learner* and international education consultant

In *She Leads*, Rachael and Majalise shine a light on the amazing work of our women in education and also the struggle of gaining access and opportunity for all women, including minorities. To learn about the worth, impact and amazingness of women leaders, read this book several times and share it with others. They will be blessed.

—**Dr. Salome Thomas-EL,** award-winning principal, speaker and author

If you are at the beginning of your career journey, this book is a must-have to set your perspective-compass in the right direction. If you are in the middle of your journey, this book is the encouragement you need to press forward and take bold steps. And if you think you may be near the end of your career journey, by the time you finish *She Leads*, you will be recharged to motivate and mentor other women by sharing the wisdom you have gained in your journey.

—**Traci Browder,** M.Ed., Intelligogy Educational Consulting

A treasure trove of strategies written with wisdom and heart. With an eclectic blend of stories, research, and practitioner voices, this book leans into the inner workings of educational leadership, covering everything from landing your first interview and navigating negotiations to embracing your strengths and connecting to others. I'm a better leader and colleague for reading this book, but I'm also excited to share the book with the women I serve alongside.

—**Dr. Brad Gustafson,** National Distinguished Principal, author, and speaker

The authors and educators featured in this book will truly inspire you to speak up and find your voice, to be proud of how far you have come, to lift up the women around you, and to "do you" the best way you know how, which is probably the best advice I've ever been given!

—**Meghan Redmond,** 2019 NASSP National Assistant
Principal of the Year

She Leads brings a multitude of perspectives to light. Regardless of where you are in your career, this is a must-add to your bookshelf.

—**Rae Hughart,** Teach Better Team

I really enjoyed the stories women in leadership shared. Every story had great strategies that were helpful. One part of the book I really connected with was the "perfection trap." I was encouraged to know I am not the only one who has struggles and challenges.

—**Rosalba Rodriguez,** elementary school principal,
Southern California

These inspiring stories prove what we know to be true: Women belong in all levels of education leadership. Together!

—**Dr. Maria Martinez-Poulin,** education leader

In *She Leads*, George and Tolan explain how men, who occupy the vast majority of superintendent positions, and school board members can help build the next generation of women leaders. Indeed, graduate degrees in educational leadership will mean very little if we do not deliberately create opportunities to apply the talent, experience, professionalism, and ingenuity that *all* of our professionals can provide.

—**Douglas Reeves,** chief executive officer,
Creative Leadership Solutions

It is true that we rise by lifting others, and Rachael and Majalise have accomplished this with *She Leads*. This book is a compilation of powerful experiences from female leaders in education that provide us with practical strategies to promote growth and success. An inspiring read for women who lead or aspire to do so.

—**Lissa Pijanowksi,** Ed. D., chief learning officer,
Innovate 2 Educate

Dr. Rachael George and Majalise Tolan are two of the very best leaders I have ever known, and their guidebook is essential reading for female leaders. *But it is also essential reading for male leaders.* Reading the guidebook helped me better understand what I can do differently to welcome women to lead as their authentic and amazing selves.

—**Craig Hawkins,** executive director, Coalition of
Oregon School Administrators

George and Tolan brilliantly inspire and wisely encourage women leaders to find their voice, to believe firmly in who they are, and to LEAD with the kind of fire that can't be put out! This is a book readers will return to again and again, no matter where they are in their leadership journey!

—**Dawn Harris,** author of *Plan Like a Pirate*

Majalise and Rachael address the tug of war that happens for women when striving to move to leadership positions while balancing work and family life. Each story inspires and empowers us to be authentic and helps us reflect on where we are in our journey and how we can continue to succeed.

—**Dr. Karen DeSouza Gallman,** director for Center for Educational
Leadership and founder of Red Lipstick Leadership

Anyone who is interested in courageous, innovative, authentic educational leadership will grow from reading this book.

—**Jay Billy,** principal and author of *Lead with Culture*

She Leads is personal, reflective, relevant, and it's going to change how you think about your own leadership. I loved this book and really think you will, too!

—**Adam Welcome,** author, podcaster,
international keynote speaker

She Leads is a must-read for all women currently serving as leaders or aspiring to be leaders. You'll feel like you're having a conversation as the authors share their vulnerable stories and impart their wisdom. Then get a copy for another friend you'd like to lift up!

—**Jessica Johnson,** principal, coauthor of *Balance Like a Pirate*

SHE LEADS

A *LEAD* Like a PIRATE *Guide*

She LEADS

The Women's Guide to a Career in
EDUCATIONAL LEADERSHIP

Dr. Rachael George   Majalise W. Tolan

She Leads: The Women's Guide to a Career in Educational Leadership
© 2022 Dr. Rachael George and Majalise W. Tolan

This book is available at special discounts when purchased in quantity for educational purposes or for use as premiums, promotions, or fundraisers. For inquiries and details, contact the publisher at books@daveburgessconsulting.com.

Published by Dave Burgess Consulting, Inc.
San Diego, CA
DaveBurgessConsulting.com

Library of Congress Control Number: 2021950419
Paperback ISBN: 978-1-956306-07-1
Ebook ISBN: 978-1-956306-08-8

Cover design and interior design by Liz Schreiter
Edited and produced by Reading List Editorial
ReadingListEditorial.com

To my incredibly strong mom, thank you for being a great role model. Your encouragement, support, and push to take risks has helped me grow into the leader I am today. I am so grateful to have you by my side.

–Rachael

To my life-long educator parents, thank you for sharing your passions with me. Athletics and the arts on the same day? Yes! To Jake, Claira, Alicenn, Jakolb, and James, thank you for understanding that my professional and personal lives often blur and being right by my side in both. Your grace allows me to lead.

–Majalise

Contents

Foreword

Being an educational leader is a challenging job. You are responsible for an almost overwhelming number of tasks. You work long hours, and even after you have left for the day, you are thinking about the work and how you can do it better. We can't help it; it is in our DNA. We want to give our best and be the best. We are natural caretakers. We take care of home, staff, students, families, the facility, crisis situations, the safety and wellbeing of others, and the list goes on. It is just what we do. Before an airplane takes off, flight attendants remind us that in emergencies we should put an oxygen mask on ourselves before helping our children or the people beside us. The message is simple: "Put YOUR mask on first." As you dive into this book and learn to lead as a woman in education, I ask that you put your mask on first. You must make it a priority to take care of yourself; then you can be fully present to LEAD.

Let me share three reasons why immersing yourself in this book is worth your precious time. First, they always say, "It is lonely at the top." Well, it does not have to be. Keep reading, and you will find that you are not alone. Our experiences are similar, no matter where you lead and no matter who you lead. It is a good feeling when you can say, "Hey, I have felt that way, too!" or "Wow, that also happened to me." You are not alone. Second, "All of us are smarter than one of us." When we put our collective experiences together, we can learn so much from each other. Be open-minded and ready to soak in some incredible knowledge from your peers. Lastly, "We are all in this together!" You are not on an island by yourself. We are truly a family, sisters on a mission to make an impact. As sisters, we share, we care, and we put our heads together to learn, grow, and make a difference on this journey. Carve time out of your busy day, flip the book open, and let's get started. Put YOUR mask on first!

Dr. Christine Handy
Past President
National Association of Secondary School Principals

Introduction

The role of women in educational leadership is constantly changing, shifting, and morphing. Because of the fluid movement of this
occupation, women have the ability to design and drive their own
career development and strengthen the role of women in education.
It is important that when these leadership moves happen they are
explicit, celebrated, and used as a model for other women to look to
and follow on their own rise in educational leadership. After all, people
believe they can do something when they see others do it before them.

Men tend to rise to positions of leadership within buildings,
schools, and districts at a much higher rate than our female peers. One
would think that with all the female teachers, especially at the elementary level, we would have more female principals, yet we don't. From
our experience, we have noticed that once they reach these positions of
leadership, men and women act very different from one another when
it comes to their leadership style.

Being a woman leader is hard. Balancing home and work life is
hard. As a group, women in leadership often talk about how we need
to support other women as they grow and lead in education; when this

support is established and recognized, it will encourage others to join. This guidebook is for women who are aspiring leaders, those navigating a variety of building and district opportunities, or those wanting to grow beyond current leadership roles. We talk about lessons learned, tips and strategies for growth, and ways to excel as a female leader.

Why I Went into Education
Rachael George

As a wildland firefighter, I fought and fought the suggestion my mother made to go into education because I thought it was too traditional and filled with too many women. My mom, an elementary principal at the time, assured me that wasn't the case, and that in many areas, men dominated the landscape. At the time, I didn't think she was telling me the complete truth, and was instead trying to rope me into something safer and more secure compared to the six months out of the year I would spend out on the fire line, out of cell service, risking my life to save natural resources and people's homes. Well, my mom was right. There were a lot of men in education, and teaching didn't have to involve applique, jumpers, and classroom decorations for each holiday. Not that those are bad, they just weren't for me.

During my first few years of teaching, I kept to the sciences and special education as they were the closest to working in the woods I could come. I showed up in Carhartts and didn't wear makeup or do my hair for three years. In fact, I remember my boss teasing me that I should at least *try* to keep the dog hair off my fleece. Slowly my Carhartts went away and were replaced with skirts, makeup began to appear, and finally I started do my hair in the morning. By the time I finished my doctorate in educational leadership and was in my first principalship, one of my supervisors noted how much I had changed and grown over the eight years since I'd first started there with my teaching license. And though I may have changed, I realized the workforce hadn't.

As a middle school principal, I was one of two secondary principals who were women in my large district. I had to relocate across the state to secure an administrative position, as it was incredibly challenging for people to move up within the district I taught in. All-administrator meetings, which were held once a month, were the only opportunities where I had a chance to interact with other women leaders. Watching and observing the dynamics during administrative meetings was fascinating just for this reason. I noticed the women held back when they had something they wanted to share. They often started their question by apologizing for interrupting or minimizing what they were about to ask. I noticed that only a few brave women would talk in front of the group and that others would feed them questions as if they were the unspoken representative. I knew I wanted to be more, model more, and lead better, so I decided to get to work learning, growing, and leading.

Why I Went into Education
Majalise Tolan

My road to education is not a surprising one. I grew up in an educator and coach home, and I learned how to grade papers and plan a practice at a very young age. My parents were teaching, supervising, watching, or coaching every event at their high schools, so the time commitment of an educator was all I knew.

I had an unrealistic and glamorous idea of what teaching entailed. I would get to engage students in subjects I was passionate about (books and history . . . how hard could that be?), attend sporting events and cheer them on, coach sports that I once loved playing, and watch my own children grow up while I was at work. None of my growing up in an educator's life prepared me for real education. I wasn't taught how to emotionally handle watching a student shake from hunger when I handed him an apple, or hear a child report something that required I call child welfare. But my favorite: nothing had prepared me for having a former student working a checkout line tell me that someone had stolen his car, and he knew who, but instead of dealing with it himself, he had called the police and let the authorities handle it just like I had always told him. Yes, the grown-up boy in the checkout line led me to tears of pride. Our students all want to make us proud. All of them, some in different ways, but they hear us and want to do what's right. Traveling as an instructional consultant across the country, I have worked with educators who hold these same beliefs. Education isn't geographical; as leaders we have a hand in setting the culture for education in our schools, districts, states, and country.

While I started my career in education already being a mother, I have come to realize this greatly impacts the work I do on a daily basis. I have moved through education with my children, as a high school assistant principal and athletic director; elementary, middle school, and high school principal; and now as a director of secondary education. As my own children have grown, I have realized that my decision-making as either a mom or an administrator blends the two worlds. I make decisions based on what I would want my own children to experience and see myself in the eyes of parents I interact with in moments of both celebration and growth—for all of us. Just like parenting, the work of a leader is never done, and it is exciting to think of where my journey will continue to take me.

This guidebook serves as a reference and support for all women leaders, regardless of where they are at in their career paths as they strive to succeed and find their voices. Together, we will explore strategies for women to take their leadership to the next level, regardless of their current or desired position.

Chapter 1

Time to Lead

The voice of women in the workplace has never been a question of *why* but a question of *when*. The time for women to lead has been and will always be now. While women account for 75 percent of teachers in the field of education, they make up only 52 percent of principals and less than 25 percent of superintendents. Of those, few are women of color—only one in ten female superintendents and two in ten female principals, according to the 2019 Chiefs for Change report.

As a collective whole, it is time to start doing something about these statistics. And that starts with knowing we belong in leadership positions that have historically been filled by men. Throw out your self-doubt, break through your imposter syndrome, and let's increase the number of women in educational leadership roles.

BELONGING

As we walked down the long hallway in the direction of my new classroom, I could smell what I would come to know as that "new school year scent"—floor wax. My heart rate increased as we approached my kindergarten classroom. I could feel the sweatiness of my grandmother's hand as she held mine ever so tight. A sense of excitement fluttered my belly. In a few seconds, I'd be meeting new friends and (finally!) learning in the "big girl school."

Just before we reached the door of my new classroom, my grandmother stopped, bent down so that her eyes were aligned with my own, and grabbed both of my shoulders. In a low voice, she stated, "This is where you belong. I don't want you to be afraid, scared, or allow anyone to make you believe otherwise." With that, I stood up a little taller, gripped my book bag handle a little tighter, and stepped into a whole new world.

My heart felt like it was going to explode.

I walked up to the only adult in the classroom. "Good morning, Miss," I said, holding out my hand for a shake. "My name is Agnella Katrise Lee and my grandmother said I belong in this class."

She looked down at me, scanned my entire being from head to toe, and sighed. "I guess so," she said, uncaring and dismissive. And then she walked away. My hand was still up in the air when I heard her directing me to a seat in the back of the room.

For the remainder of the day, I recall looking down at my hands, my blue-plaid jumper dress, my neatly positioned white socks, and my Buster Brown shoes just to make sure I was truly present. I belonged at school, right? Year after year, I faced recurring thoughts of whether or not I truly belonged.

On many occasions, I allow that thought to lurk in my head, or I find myself questioning my belonging in professional settings as a K–12 superintendent. Currently, I am the only African American superintendent out of 197 districts in Oregon. Naturally, when I look around at my colleagues, I question myself about belonging.

Almost fifteen years ago, a dear colleague offered a piece of advice that I tap into regularly. Her words are clear even today: "How you present yourself, that is important. And how you see yourself is even more important."

This world is massive, and if you plan to lead in any capacity then you must begin to believe that you belong. There will be times you doubt your place, so you have to fake it until you make it. Work at it and claim a sense of belonging in time.

Welcome to educational leadership. There's seat at the table just for you—go ahead, take it. As my grandmother reminded me on my first day of school: This is where you belong. I don't want you to be afraid, scared, or allow anyone to make you believe otherwise.

Dr. A. Katrise Perera

STRATEGIES:

- Leading isn't always comfortable or welcoming. Don't be afraid or scared; lean in.
- Hold your head high, no matter how folks treat you.
- You must begin to believe you belong.

Some female leaders have shared that they feel lonely when leading. When they get to this point, waves of doubt can still come over them, even when deep down they know their worth and passions. It is important that when that happens, they focus on their strengths, passions, and desire to do and be more in the field of education. As Dr. Karen Gray said, "Education is hard work. What you give, you give as an extension of yourself, your soul. A big part of my personality was molded by having to be tough, to stand up for what was right even when I knew that I would appear to be a 'bitch.' I did it anyway and my students and their families benefited from my loud advocacy." This advocacy Gray references is possible when leaders lead with their heads held high and believe in their self-worth in their leadership roles.

KNOW YOUR WORTH

I am worthy. I had to remind myself of this each day when I was hired for my first administrator job. In a majority white school district, I was the only administrator or teacher of color in the entire building.

I was a smart, educated, knowledgeable person. I'd earned the administrator position because of my experience. I'd worked hard to achieve this goal. However, as a person of color, I felt that my colleagues wondered why I was hired.

The doubts set in after I engaged with staff members. As one colleague told me in the beginning of the school year, I was "just different." The staff had never had a person of color as an administrator, my colleague explained. I was perplexed: Was it really so different for staff, simply because of the color of my skin?

I found myself being more reserved, quiet and at times nervous because I did not want to say the wrong thing. The feeling was very foreign to me. My teaching experience had been in a majority school district of color. While there, I had been confident in my abilities, felt comfortable, and made a connection with children who mirrored me when I was a young child. I wanted to be an administrator so I could effect change in our schools and make decisions that were in the best interest of students and families.

Was I doubting myself because of how others felt about me? Why did I let their feelings or viewpoints impact who I was and how I behaved?

One day in my office, I gave myself a talking-to. "This is not you," I said. "Be you!" Leading as myself looked like this: being assertive, sharing my voice and experience, asking poignant questions, engaging in conversations with colleagues, challenging staff to find ways to best meet the individual needs of students, and, yes, being confident in myself. I deserved this position. I was hired to bring about change. And I could not let other people's perceptions of me sway me from my purpose.

Once I began leading as my authentic self, a weight lifted off of my shoulders. I was able to appreciate my own voice as I worked to support the students and families in my school, regardless of their race or ethnicity. Some may say I speak my mind too openly, and, ironically, I take that as a compliment. I will never go back to self-doubt. I am worthy. My voice matters and must be heard to be a beacon of change for my students.

My courage paid off. Later that school year, the staff member who told me that it was different having me as an administrator praised me for my advocacy and intuitiveness and said, "I am so happy that you are here." Those words taught me how important it is to be true to myself at all times.

Since then, I have never let my self-confidence wane. As I work with new administrators, one of the main things I teach them is to be confident in themselves and their convictions. I say the same to you now. You matter. Your voice matters. And your perspective matters.

> *You matter. Your voice matters.*
> *And your perspective matters.*
>
> — *Beverly Green*

STRATEGIES:

- Present ideas you are passionate about and committed to.
- Share your perspective so the female voice is heard.
- Learn from everyone in the room. Invite their questions and ideas.
- Sometimes our ideas or views aren't in line with the majority. Advocate for your beliefs, evaluate your next steps, and reflect. Know when to push and when to let go.

—————————— *Majalise's Story* ——————————

MAKE ROOM FOR OTHER WOMEN

You're in a leadership position—congrats! But your work's not done. Women leaders are also charged with encouraging more women to channel their leadership potential to new positions. There's no limit to the number of women who can fill leadership roles, so let's support other women in getting there.

Once, I had the opportunity to interview a former colleague for a leadership position in our district. She did well, but having known her from my former job, I knew she had so much more to offer a district. I also recognized some gaps in her interview that clued me in on areas where she could grow. At this point, I had two choices: hope she didn't call to ask for honest feedback or reach out and offer to help her grow.

I ended up reaching out to her and asking if she wanted to debrief the interview. We talked about some professional growth opportunities to strengthen her background and ways to improve her interview for the next round. I also offered a follow-up call to talk through potential job opportunities and to help strengthen her background knowledge in moving to a new district. When she let me know that she had been hired for her first administrator position, I might have been just as excited as she was! Supporting other women as they move along their career paths is just as rewarding as moving yourself. Together, we can do more.

WELCOMING WOMEN

The world of athletics is dominated by male leadership. As a female leader in a world of male coaches and athletic directors, I'm keenly aware of how far women have come—and how much further we have to go.

We have a responsibility to our fellow women to urge educational, athletic, and community organizations to consider the inclusion of diverse leaders, including women. Intentionally lifting other women to leadership positions and mentoring those who have yet to find their voice has to be part of the process. That's why, in my role as an assistant executive director at the Oregon School Activities Association, I have tried to welcome other women into athletics leadership. Their experiences are diverse, and the collaboration is rich. I look forward to female-focused discussions when we connect with one another and find ways to enrich our work environments.

— K. T. Emerson

STRATEGIES:

- Identify and remove barriers that prevent women from accessing leadership opportunities.
- Recruit and hire women for your staff.
- Invite women to networking events and collaboration opportunities.
- Celebrate women and their accomplishments.

FIND YOUR VOICE

Many of us have been there: looking at a social media post, listening to a TED talk or interview, or simply reading a magazine wondering how *she* can be so confident and speak her truth. We fall prey to our perception without exploring or learning more about that particular woman's story. I know this to be true, because as I reflect on my own journey, I must confess I can recall many moments when I questioned where other women's success came from and if I would ever be able to stand for something worthy. I had allowed a negative voice to create false narratives about my purpose, shutting off a much-needed message worthy of sharing. For years I felt that there was no place for me to be an agent of change for minority students and Latina leaders. Many times, I feared that engaging in these conversations would be too much and questioned if I was the right person to advocate for these causes. Inside, my heart was overflowing with a desire to speak; however, the mind played a soundtrack that kept me from speaking my truth, from sharing the voice within.

Discovering your voice is not about being loud or radical. It is all about being open and staying true to your beliefs and the causes you stand for. It is about letting others know where you draw the line, your boundaries, your message, what you stand for, and the compelling "why" that keeps you up at night. Your voice will become your most powerful weapon because, if used well, it will allow you to send a clear message that can change mindsets, conversations, and narratives around what you stand for. Discovering my voice has allowed me to learn over the years that there is power in a strong "yes" and a strong "no" when it comes to my values, and that I can still do this in ways that show respect and kindness to others. When we know our purpose and look for ways to influence others with our message, we make everyone around us wonder where that confidence came from and how they can become more like us. Fear no longer holds us prisoner and we can use our voice to effect real change.

One of the ways I like to build on these skills is engaging in daily reflection. Every morning I go over my schedule, looking at meetings and collaboration opportunities with different stakeholders. Not only does this help me prepare for the day, but it also lets me know the spaces I will be in where I can be an advocate for students or be the voice for the organization I work for. Knowing my role in these spaces allows me to prepare and be intentional about my message and about how it can add value to the conversation, but also to challenge others' thinking about issues that matter for some of our most vulnerable student groups. Knowing and anticipating how I can be present allows me to grow in this area. It helps me go beyond passion and step confidently into my purpose as I am invited into different spaces. Most importantly, it helps me stand in my truth, letting others know what my values are.

Just remember that finding your voice is not about proving your worth to others; instead, your worth will prove to be what will bring strength to your voice. As you reflect daily, become intentional about it. Make everyone around you wonder where that powerful and amazing voice came from. Be a gift to others and share the message many other women need to hear. We are all waiting. We all need it. Will it be easy? Probably not. However, I can guarantee it will be totally worth it. Kick insecurity to the curb and make room for a voice that will change this world.

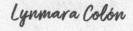

Lynmara Colón

STRATEGIES:

- Social media is great but it can do a number on your confidence. Know when to tune it out.
- Remember, you are a change agent and students need your voice!
- Know your purpose.
- Engage in daily reflection.

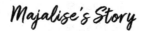

SPEAK UP

When I moved to a new district for a building administrative position, I wanted to replicate a professional-development institute I had attended. After discussing, our curriculum director asked me to pitch the idea to district leadership. I felt comfortable around the team in a less formal setting, but was nervous presenting to the entire cabinet.

My stressed-out brain didn't record much of that meeting, but I do remember this: When asked a logistical question, I fumbled the answer. It felt like a neon sign lit over my head, flashing "She Doesn't Belong Here." But instead of judging me for not knowing the answer, our superintendent stepped in to help, noting that the logistical detail was something we'd need to work out. Being in a collaborative setting where my voice was encouraged helped me be okay with not having all of the answers.

I have found that it can be difficult for women to feel like they belong—especially when they're new to a district. So women stay quiet, holding back ideas and opinions. But when new ideas, concerns, or possible solutions are not shared, the district loses. Remember: You were hired for a reason. Speaking your truth, contributing to the improvement of the district, and working with others is critical for success. Women strive for leadership positions to be part of the change, so why wait?

Remember: You were hired for a reason.

If you are struggling to find your voice, that's okay. We have both been there before. Sometimes it has been due to our being in a new setting, other times it has been because we have a viewpoint different than others'. And yes, we even struggle with confidence at times. During these moments of despair, we have found it is still valuable for us to share our voice. When our stomach drops and our heartbeat quickens, we know we need to speak up. One strategy that is helpful for us is Mel Robbins's 5 Second Rule, where you count down from five and then you jump in. This strategy is great for speaking up or helping generate momentum with anything where you struggle just to get started. When it's uncomfortable, we sometimes add the lines "Here's a thought . . ." or "What do you think?" to help offset the idea. This throws the idea out to the group or other party without coming across confrontational. Finally, know that it's okay to disagree without being disagreeable. As long as you acknowledge the other perspective and professionally and respectfully give your opinion, you are good.

The time for women to lead is now. We must conquer our self-doubt and know that we belong. Women in leadership have an obligation to expand female voice and representation throughout the many roles educational leaders hold. By encouraging women to be bold in sharing their ideas and supporting each other in their necessary development to be hired in leadership positions, we will move beyond having women in only 25 percent of superintendent roles.

CHART YOUR COURSE

⚓ What self-doubt do you need to identify and work through on your leadership path? Who can help you build that confidence?

⚓ How can you build intentional reflection time into your schedule? What is one area of focus you would like to reflect on daily that will help you on your career path?

Chapter 2

It's a Career Jungle Gym

I f you've thought about your professional future, you've probably envisioned a career ladder that will help you rise from where you are now to where you'd like to be. In education, metaphorical career ladders explain the steps you must take to advance your career. For example, you must be a teacher before you can become a principal, or, if your dream job is to become superintendent, you'll need to serve as both teacher and principal first. It's nice in theory, but limiting in practice.

It is time we ditch the career ladder. In order to get more women into leadership roles, we have to throw out the traditional, linear way of thinking when it comes to career advancement. Think "jungle gym" instead.

Sheryl Sandberg describes it best in her book *Lean In:* "Ladders are limiting—people can move up or down, on or off. . . . The jungle gym model benefits everyone, especially women who might be starting careers, switching careers, getting blocked by external barriers, or reentering the workforce after taking time off."

This approach gives you freedom to play around, moving from the swings to the slide but skipping the sandbox. Or, in career terms, moving from a vice principal position to being a district office administrator but skipping building principal. Or when a special education teacher becomes a special education director at the district office. There are many examples of unique paths women in leadership have taken—like a director of human resources who hasn't worked in education before. Just ask around.

Career advice is great, but only you know the best path for you. We encourage you to crawl, climb, and grow through leadership positions, hurtle over roadblocks, and challenge the naysayers. While colleagues, and even friends, may say you are not qualified or skilled enough to lead, don't be discouraged. You can, will, and are doing it.

Majalise's Story

MIND YOUR KNOWLEDGE GAPS

My first job as an administrator was as a high school assistant principal and athletic director. One day, our superintendent called and asked me to cover a maternity leave at an elementary school. I was scared for one major reason: I did not have any experience at that age level. But my assistant superintendent, who was a former elementary principal of the year, would support me through this learning curve, and I'd return to my old job in a few months. This approach seemed great because I loved the high school and was hesitant to leave.

Working at the elementary school was exhilarating. Just like at the high school, I put in long hours, but I could do a lot of my learning, studying, and reading when my own kids were in bed. Overall, the teachers were amazing, as they welcomed my questions when I hung out in their classrooms, challenged me, supported me, and provided me feedback.

In the end, my worries about being unqualified were unfounded. By working to fill gaps in my knowledge, I was able to make a successful transition. Not only that, but I became a better secondary administrator because I saw students through a whole new lens when I returned to the high school.

A unique career path has its strengths—it provides flexibility and creativity—but if you're following one, know your limitations. Be aware of knowledge gaps. For female leaders, who have historically had a background in curriculum and instruction, the knowledge gap between finance and management could be something to consider. For example, if you haven't been a building principal yourself but now supervise building principals, you'll need to learn and listen to their roles and responsibilities in order to understand your staff's challenges and needs, which may be both personal and professional. Or if you oversee an athletic director and haven't served in that role before, you might have some learning ahead of you to understand an athletic director's role and expected workload. As you move through the career jungle gym, determine where you have gaps in knowledge, then fill them in.

> Determine where you have gaps in knowledge, then fill them in.

There are plenty of ways to learn the necessary skills of the job. We invite you to listen to those around you or in your network and be humbly aware you don't know everything. Perhaps you can ask those you lead, and research and learn about roles you haven't held that are historically held by men, such as the superintendent or athletic director. Or maybe even go back to school for continuing education classes.

THERE IS NO RIGHT LEADERSHIP PATH OR POSITION

"I have no idea what I am doing!" I said to myself within the first couple weeks of my new job in a medium-sized K–12 school district. I was being groomed to move into the human resources director position under the mentorship of my superintendent. My transition into the role took about ten months, and a huge chunk of the job—the concepts, processes, systems, and general education lingo—was new to me.

I had a bachelor's degree in human resource management, had worked in the private sector as a director for five years, and spent seven years as a coordinator/specialist. Neither my education nor experience had prepared me for the high stakes of making decisions in accordance with board policies, labor contracts, the Teacher Standards and Practices Commission rules, and Oregon Administrative Rules that govern contracts, evaluation, discipline, and termination.

I needed help. A respected colleague shared their belief that education is one of the most hierarchical organizations in our society and told me it would benefit me to get my administrative license, even if just for the clout it gives one with fellow administrators and teacher union leaders. Therefore, I made a personal decision to seek out a state administrator licensing program, which is the same program principals go through.

In my quest to learn the ways of education administration, I got a master's in education administration and my initial administrator's license—within a year and a half, while working in my position full-time, and being a full-time mom of three. Most of my coursework forced me to think and act like a principal and I was required to spend several hours interning as a principal in both elementary and secondary environments. This gave me keen insight that comes in handy when working with, supporting, and conducting performance or disciplinary processes.

When Oregon's Senate Bill 290 (Educator Effectiveness) was passed, increasing the requirements for teacher and administrator evaluation, I spent hours learning the Danielson Evaluation Instrument (Framework for Teaching) and became a Danielson trainer along with my colleagues. I was immersed in this world, and it helped me truly understand that "every child can learn," and, as in my case, every adult can, too.

Not following the "right" career ladder has made it difficult to prove myself in certain circles, but for the most part, I have gained the confidence of the administrators I support in both districts I have worked in. In fact, they heavily depend on me.

— *Chelsi Reno*

STRATEGIES:

- Have confidence when others believe in you, and rely on their mentorship.
- Seek out specific forms of professional development that will support your career aspirations.
- Gain credibility by learning in the field. Don't be afraid to learn from those around you or those you supervise.
- Embrace the challenge and expand your application of job-related skills.

Leading from Anywhere

While we are climbing the jungle gym of educational leadership, it is important to remember that not all leaders leave the classroom or certified teaching ranks. Some may become teacher mentors or teachers on special assignment working in data or curriculum and instruction. Others may take on the responsibility of becoming a model classroom teacher that embodies exemplar systems, structures, best instructional and behavioral practices, and classroom community.

Don't be afraid to reassess your definition of leadership. Maybe you spent years working toward becoming an instructional coach. Maybe you even landed the job but found your calling is working directly with students on a daily basis. An in-classroom role may veer from the career path you imagined, but it could be just what you need to feel fulfilled. Women leaders are needed in all aspects of education leadership to improve the system.

LEADERS AREN'T JUST AT THE TOP

I made it to the so-called top: principal of an elementary school with forty-four staff. Yet my passion, strength, and journey led me back to the ground floor with the kids. As soon as I realized my true calling, I jumped in with both feet. I accepted a position at a structured learning center that had four staff and nineteen kids between fourth and sixth grade, and was granted an emergency teaching license in special education. It was like a school within a school—and it required a leader.

I had a day to prep with my team, which I filled by reviewing individual education plans and learning this new team's common language, expectations, and strategies. I had a clear vision for staff and students, and with consistency, follow through, and constant teaching of staff and students, we became the model classroom within a year.

Staff no longer struggled with the procedures and processes because they saw these work for the students. The results were energizing. Students no longer struggled with school, because they were given an opportunity to learn in an environment where their needs were understood and where they and their futures were valued and cared for.

Leaders are not just for "the top" of the career ladder. If students are going to have true and meaningful learning year after year, we need a leader at each step of the way. Creating a successful learning environment and program fills my heart with pride as I watched the students grow and achieve. This is what motivates me—directly impacting student growth. This is what makes me feel like I am "at the top."

— *Pedra Weber*

STRATEGIES:

- Don't be afraid to follow your occupational passion. Leaders fill all roles.
- Jump in and lead. When you get the chance, go for it!
- Implement your vision. It isn't always easy, but consistency and communication are key for any leader.
- Positive results are energizing. Celebrate them!

Rachael's Story

USING THE JUNGLE GYM

One day, I would love to be a superintendent. Right now, I truly love my job as an executive director of student services, elementary programs, and pre-K principal, and my current state of work-life balance. When my husband retires, I will be ready to take that leap. Knowing I have six years or fewer before doing so, I am taking steps now toward my goal as I move throughout the jungle gym. I've identified specific skills and leadership abilities that I need to develop, which has allowed me to seek out opportunities for growth, as well as guidance, support, and mentorship from others in these leadership positions above and around me. I can use everything I learn when I make my future move.

While you might love your job and have no interest in jumping to the next level, keep your long-term career plans within your sights. And, yes, long-term planning fits into the career jungle gym—just in a different way. Instead of mapping out the exact jobs you'll need to hold to land your dream job, approach future planning from a skills-based mindset. You can move sideways in your career provided you hold the right skills for the job. Think of it like watching the rest of the playground while you're on the swings.

As leadership experts Sally Helgesen and Marshall Goldsmith discuss in their book *How Women Rise*, women tend to be driven by loyalty. It's a good quality to have, but in the workplace, loyalty can lead to roadblocks. The desire to be loyal can lead women to avoid looking for other jobs, stifle ambition needed to advance within a company, neglect future planning, and sell their talent short. In education, you might be deeply loyal to your boss, your district, or your team.

Regardless of how happy you are in your job, take a step back and reflect on your career goals and your ideal timeframes for making transitions. Be visible in the organization, create connections with others and make sure they know you are up for a challenge, and talk to your boss about your long-term desires. If you aren't talking about the future of your career, they might not be thinking about it.

OPEN TO OPPORTUNITIES

As a consultant for over seventeen years, I have had many opportunities to meet other educators, most of them women, as they engage in professional learning and navigate their roles. Some of them are unhappy in their current positions. Some of them are looking for new challenges. Many of them are impressive, and from my outsider perspective, they are being underutilized in their current positions.

At a train-the-trainer event years ago, I met a woman named Denise. Like so many of the women I work with, she was a total rock star—someone I knew would shape education in important ways. Denise was an instructional coach who had attended several of my professional learning sessions over the course of a year.

She also ended up in one of my certification trainings. Throughout the three-day course, I became more and more impressed by her practice presentations, interactions with colleagues, and insightful comments. When the time came for her to give her final presentation, I was blown away. She could've taken my place in the company the very next day; she was just that good. I don't recall the exact feedback I gave her after the presentation, but I remember commenting on the broad impact she could have on other educators and suggesting she consider how she wanted to use her immense talent.

Recently, Denise and I reconnected for a virtual conference that her consulting company sponsored. That's right: Over several years, she worked her way from instructional coach to cofounder of a consulting company that recently held an online event for 5,000 attendees, with keynotes from some of the biggest names in educational research. What a journey! As she introduced me to attendees, she shared the story of that long-ago presentation. She said that my feedback helped her rethink her career path and launch her current venture.

Despite what you may believe, the most important part of my role as a consultant is not the expertise I bring. It is my ability to help folks see what is possible. When I ask educators genuine questions about their roles and what effects they hope to have in their school systems, I do it to prompt them to think clearly and actively about their career goals.

Whether you love your job or are biding your time until you get a promotion, be careful not to become stagnant. Consider possible ways you can inspire other educators, then keep moving forward. The journey they take from there may be part of their original career path or, like it was for Denise, a detour to an unexpected opportunity.

Angela Peery

STRATEGIES:

- Use feedback as a way to encourage women to do more with their strengths and grow professionally.
- Leverage your leadership abilities to help others see what is possible on their own path.
- Ask questions and prompt others to think about their own career goals.
- Don't fall into the professional trap of becoming stagnant. Follow your career path and don't fear a detour.

There is no one right career path. For women in education, leadership may come slowly, quickly, in a straight line, or in a zig-zag—and that's totally fine! The important thing is to embrace the journey, infuse it with reflection, and commit to bridging your knowledge gaps. Every occupation in education is full of leaders: those willing to step up, step out, and lead by example. Never underestimate or devalue your path to the leadership position you desire. Remember, when we were kids, we ran to the jungle gym and never wanted to get off.

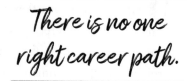

There is no one right career path.

CHART YOUR PATH

⚓ What knowledge gaps do you need to fill to move along your career path? What leaders and resources will help you learn and grow?

⚓ Education is filled with many occupations that complete the system. In what areas do you see yourself as a leader, and how would you like to lead?

Chapter 3

The Power of Emotion

R aise your hand if you've heard someone describe women leaders as "emotional." Research by Daniel Goleman, author of *Emotional Intelligence*, shows that when it comes to men versus women, our brains function differently, so this makes sense. When faced with emotion, men sense the feeling for a moment and then they move on to problem-solving. Women, on the other hand, tend to stay with those emotional feelings much longer. Even with our brain functioning a little different, it is time we stood up against the stereotype of the emotional woman leader as a negative trait. Yes, leaders are supposed to be solid, steadfast, and calm during a storm. Good leaders, however, can also be passionate, assertive, and intense. In fact, we have observed strong, incredible women leaders harness the power of emotion to reach new heights.

We have both been told that there are good and bad emotions when it comes to leadership. It is good to be fired up, motivated, happy, and inspired. We have also been told it is not okay to cry, show you care, or display your emotions. Over time, we have found it *is* okay to show your emotional side; in fact, we believe it makes you more relatable, human, and authentic in your leadership. So while you might be afraid to show your emotions as a leader, know that when you let your guard down and start showing up as yourself, emotions and all, you truly start living in alignment with who you are.

EMBRACING EMOTIONS

I am not afraid to admit I am one of those people who cries during Hallmark commercials and often tears up when reading stories to my students. Over the years, I have slowly learned to acknowledge my emotions, share my emotions, and accept that I am an emotional person.

I am also an emotional leader. That's not a derogatory term. Emotions have been a surprising boon to my career.

Like the time I was fired up about a staffing issue while talking to a male union rep. I broke down in the meeting and cried—then apologized to the man who witnessed me in an extremely vulnerable state. But I felt like by showing my passion and how I truly felt, he knew I was being completely honest. Our conversation reached a new level. He knew exactly where I was coming from because I had exposed my emotional thinking. At that moment, I was not being emotional. I was being an emotional leader.

Then there were the times I gave in to emotions following a series of losses before I successfully got pregnant. My staff certainly knew I was experiencing sadness, often privately, and that being a female leader of a school full of little children was extremely tough for me. Once I even had to leave school to go straight to the hospital for emergency surgery, on open house night of all times. My staff jumped in and was there for me and the school when I couldn't be the visible leader. I don't believe that would have happened if I had not been so vulnerable, if I had not presented myself as someone who led with my heart, not just my head.

When talking about vulnerability and emotional thinking, I have to mention Brené Brown and the impact her words had on me as an "emotional thinker" and female leader. When I read "Who we are is how we lead" in her book *Dare To Lead,* I couldn't help but pump my fist and cheer out loud. I am an emotional thinker. That is who I am, and that is how I lead.

Never has my emotions-driven leadership style been clearer than during the COVID-19 closure. My focus during every remote meeting with my staff centered on the mental state of our students, staff, and families. We may not have been physically together, but we became more connected than ever during the school closure. I was vulnerable with my staff, opening up about my worries, my fears, my frustrations, and my grief. That didn't make me a weak leader; if their messages of gratitude are anything to go by, it made me a *better* leader.

I was also vulnerable with my students' parents. I shared weekly video updates in which I was very honest, sharing what our remote learning life was like in my own house. I cried when talking about how I was frustrated that I was losing my patience with my own children. I cried when I talked to parents about how we need to address our current school climate and educate ourselves and our children about racism. I even kept the video rolling when I got upset with my child for interrupting me. Was I weak? Unprofessional? To the contrary. After each video, I received numerous emails from parents and staff thanking me for being so honest. They did not see me as a weak, emotional female leader. They saw me as a real human, an emotionally brave leader, and a parent whose experiences were just like theirs.

As a female leader, I will always choose to lead with my head *and* my heart. I won't keep my emotions hidden; I will acknowledge them and let them guide me.

Liz Garden

STRATEGIES:

- Instead of working to keep your emotions hidden from others, try expressing how you feel and how situations impact you.
- Work to let your guard down and connect with your families, students, and staff.
- We are all human and life happens. Instead of acting like everything is perfect and you have your act together, just own wherever you are at in life.
- Just show up. Be unapologetically, authentically you.

HARNESSING YOUR MAMA BEAR

The best part of being an educator for the last twenty years is that I never stop learning and growing. Some of my most memorable moments have been when my students remind me of something I've taught them and, in the process, end up teaching me.

Recently, our state student-leadership organization received some not-so-kind Instagram messages. I knew I needed to wait to respond; however, the mama bear urge to protect my students took over. I responded quickly and was quite straightforward and defensive in my response. I had sent a few messages back and forth with the person who had posted on social media when my phone dinged with a text from a student:

Student: At student executive council, we talked and decided to use the twenty-four-hour rule when responding to comments, just so emotions are not involved.

Me: I needed that reminder. Thank you! I get so passionate and protective. Patience is not a strength of mine.

Student: I'm so glad we are all working together on this. Multiple brains and perspectives are always better.

I was reminded of a lesson I had learned years before, when a nasty email from a student's father had me shooting off a defensive email that led to—surprise—another nasty email. My principal aptly described what it's like to hit send in a rush: you instantly feel relief and then you have a mess to clean up.

— *Sara Nilles-Freauf*

STRATEGIES:

- Don't be afraid to learn from your students. They just might be modeling your teaching.
- When feeling a negative response to an email, don't rush to hit send. Give yourself and the sender time to reflect on the initial communication before continuing.
- Reread your email before sending. You can respond straightforwardly without being defensive. Tone of email is just as important as tone of voice.

— *Rachael's Story* —

IT'S OKAY TO NOT BE OKAY

As leaders, we are often faced with the challenge of appearing like we have our act together and are made of emotional steel. Many of us have been trained to hide our feelings for fear of being viewed as weak, emotional, or incompetent. While we may believe we are doing the right thing by putting up this emotional wall or barrier, we are actually doing a disservice to both ourselves and those we lead. Hiding your feelings isn't authentic leadership. Be present in each moment by acknowledging your emotions.

Let's say you're dealing with a child abuse situation and it makes your stomach turn, or with the unexpected departure of a staff member due to cancer. Maybe you are feeling sad, helpless, or out of control. Don't push your emotions away. Instead, work through them:

1. Take a deep breath and know that everything will be okay.
2. Name the emotion you're experiencing.
3. Acknowledge or identify why the emotion exists.
4. Identify the impact the emotion has at the current moment and the work that needs to be done.
5. Make a plan to move forward through this grief cycle so you can process the emotions in a healthy way.
6. Give yourself time to step away from the situation and find someone to connect with.

During my first year as an elementary principal, I found myself sitting in my office crying. I was frustrated and incredibly exhausted. Try to picture it: my head on the desk, tears running down my face, blotchy skin.

When a teacher popped into my office to ask a quick question, I was mortified. It was after school hours and I had thought most of the staff had gone home for the evening. Nope. As quickly as I could, I lifted my head, wiped my face, and mumbled something about allergies. I'm sure the teacher didn't buy the lie, but she continued on as if she didn't see my tears and red, puffy eyes.

I may not have realized it then, but I do now: It is okay to cry and show emotion—even as a leader. Don't beat yourself up for letting your guard down. You are a real person with real feelings, so when emotions bubble up and the tears start to form, let yourself feel. (And try one of the tips below.)

> *Don't beat yourself up for letting your guard down.*

WHEN YOU'RE NOT OKAY, TRY THIS:

- Take some deep breaths.
- Turn on a meditation or mindfulness app (we love Peloton's app).
- Take a walk.
- Visit a classroom. Kids have a way of making us smile.
- Take a break. Work will still be there when you return.
- Call a friend or colleague so you can talk through the situation and gain perspective.
- Keep an item, such as a brain-teaser or puzzle, accessible in your office. Work on it when your brain needs a break.

Emotional struggle is a real thing. Often leaders, especially women, trying to show they can lead without emotion, will work hard to deliberately cover up their emotions and keep that personal and human side of their self hidden from professional view. However, doing this for too long can not only build an emotional barrier between leaders and staff, it can also make it even more difficult for staff to handle when that breaking point of vulnerability comes and a leader unexpectedly shows their emotions.

Showing emotion is okay. As immersed leaders, we all feel the weight of the staff and students we care about. Our decisions have weight not just on those they directly impact, but on those of us making and carrying out the decisions. Sometimes, those decisions or events happen to us and we are in a position to react, just like those we are leading. When it happens, our emotions may show, and that is a powerful sign of authentic leadership.

ADMITTING YOU'RE STRUGGLING

March 13, 2020, will forever be etched in my brain. That day, we sent students home a week early for spring break. What we'd thought would be an extended vacation turned into a year of remote learning in order to avoid the spread of COVID-19.

I was in a constant state of worry, scanning social media, watching the news, and waking during the night to updates about the virus's quick spread. If my phone was not sending me news, I went in search of it. I'd awaken in the middle of the night to search for updates. I was afraid of the virus making its way to my community. And I was stressed about how it was impacting the school.

As a principal, you cannot help but worry about the academic well-being of students, but you also find yourself worrying about the social, emotional, and nutritional well-being of each and every child from your school. All of that was on my mind during the pandemic, but so was the safety and well-being of my staff, some of whom are single and young, living away from their immediate family. Others had underlying health issues that made them medically vulnerable. By the end of March, I could only be described as depressed.

For the first time in my life, I was finding that I was not so resilient. I cannot clearly articulate how I felt—in all honesty, I tried hard not to identify what I was feeling. I found myself struggling to care for my daughter and husband, much less myself. Manage supplemental learning for my fourth grader while leading a building involved in an emergency response to a pandemic? I was not doing any of it well, and my own child was paying the greatest price as I focused hard on my school. Mentally and emotionally, I was sinking fast.

Things began to shift when I admitted publicly that I was struggling. It happened in a virtual meeting with administrators from my school district. Our superintendent asked how we were doing—how we were *really* doing. I wish I could recall what motivated me to speak up. My superintendent is a powerful presence. She is dedicated and cares deeply about every aspect of our school district. I am not an aspiring superintendent, but in many ways, I would like to be her when I "grow up." Perhaps the fact that she checks in with principals often meant I trusted the sincerity in her question. Whatever it was, I was scared to be so completely vulnerable, and yet that was when my healing began. I laid it out for everyone to see: I was struggling. After a moment of silence, my peers responded compassionately. They were struggling, too.

Leaders are only human. We experience life just like everyone else, with ups and downs. It's okay to have moments when we aren't okay. When folks ask how you are doing, be honest with them. In sharing, we open ourselves up to deeper relationships with others.

Kristin Takano Becker

STRATEGIES:

- Being an emotional leader is not the same as being emotional. The emotional vulnerability in decision-making can be powerful.
- When the situation fits, don't be afraid to show staff and families how your own life is impacted by your educational organization.
- Don't perpetuate the myth that leaders always have it all together. Sometimes we struggle at home, at work, or with a decision. Lean on your school community.
- Your own honesty in times of struggle may be exactly what others need to hear to let their guard down and release themselves to transparency when they are struggling, too.

Majalise's Story

THE ONLY WAY OUT OF GRIEF IS THROUGH

Situations that bring out the most emotion in leaders are often those we weren't taught about in educational leadership programs. Crises are crash courses in emotional leadership. When times are toughest, we're forced to balance own our emotions with leading others through the crisis.

For me, this came in the form of a student death. For leaders in charge of a school full of children, grief is a reality that cannot be checked at the door.

The first time I dealt with the death of a student, it was a little girl who had played with my daughter during parent teacher conferences just days before. I had to walk into a room full of children and tell them their friend, who had been sick with cancer, had died. It was the hardest conversation I had ever had with students, to the point that I didn't even remember it when I walked out of the room. As I left, I asked my district support team how it went. They both looked at me and said, "It was perfect. Do it again." The problem was, I had no idea what I had said. My heart and faith spoke to those students. I became their mother and wanted to hold them and speak to them like I would my own children—I told the truth and, together, we sat in the moment.

At the time, my idea of work-life balance verged on unhealthy, and the death tipped it over the edge. I would call my husband each night to make sure my kids were in bed before I came home. The thought of going home to four healthy children while a family in our school community was grieving the loss of their daughter was too much for me to handle. I was an absolute mess because I was doing everything I could to hold it together at work and to be strong for my students, staff, and school.

My own children needed me, and I needed them, too. I will never forget the first time I came home while my kids were awake. Our youngest, just two at the time, climbed on my lap. He didn't speak and he didn't need to. Our children know when we are hurting, and they want to help.

The same was true for the children at my school. Near the end of the student's funeral, a young boy approached me while I silently cried off to the side—my feeble attempt at going unnoticed. He gave me a big hug and said, "It is okay, Ms. Tolan. It is all going to be okay."

Through this experience, I learned that it is okay to cry in front of kids. Or that if you feel you can't be vulnerable at school, then make sure to give yourself time once you get home. If you find yourself dealing with grief in your school, know it will be okay. Find someone to talk to for your own emotional sake: a trusted friend, colleague, counselor, pastor, or another leader who has been in the same position. Your partner or spouse will be watching you grieve, so be sure they have someone to talk to if needed.

Sadly, this first time losing a student has not been the last time in my career. It has never gotten easier, and I have never been prepared. I have learned, though, that being vulnerable with staff and students is healthy. Just like we model instructional practices, assembly behavior, and fire drill procedures, we have the opportunity as leaders to appropriately model emotional pain. Entering the care room with students and taking a moment to write a memory is not just good for modeling, but it helps you take that moment to be with your community and to be part of the grieving process, not a bystander leading it. Taking the time today to identify who can help during times of tragedy in your school, professional life, and personal life will ease the emotional stress on everyone involved if grief occurs. And knowing and accepting that we will all handle it differently is important.

Emotions are powerful and a strength for women in leadership. They help women relate and connect to those around them. Emotions should not be feared, but realized, identified, and processed. Leaders who hide emotions hide a part of their authentic self that is essential in making decisions and building relationships. Learning to use emotions is critical to becoming a stronger leader.

CHART YOUR PATH

⚓ How have your used or witnessed emotions as leader? What would you do the same and what would you change in the future?

⚓ Who can you use as a sounding board or check-and-connect when emotions are high? What makes that relationship important when working through your emotions?

Chapter 4

Landing the Job

For many women, applying for a new job goes something like this: Discover the Perfect Job. Experience crushing self-doubt. Scour the job posting for indicators that we are qualified for Perfect Job. Mentally check off the posting's list of qualifications. Experience wave two of self-doubt. Determine we meet all job qualifications. Apply.

Men, on the other hand, look at the list of job qualifications as a guideline and wish list. In fact, a 2014 *Harvard Business Review* article by Tara Sophia Mohr discussed a Hewlett-Packard internal report which found that men, on average, apply to jobs when they meet 60 percent of the qualifications, while women only apply when they are a 100 percent match.

One of the hardest parts of finding a job is working up the nerve to apply. We get it: Submitting your first application is scary. The prospect of rejection is petrifying, and many of us internalize the rejection and equate it to our professional and personal self-worth. Fear has a way of stifling success. After all, you won't get rejected if you don't apply—but you also won't get the job. We are here to tell you that if you aren't careful, fear will hold you back. We have both had those moments—until we decided to get after it! We encourage you not to let your insecurities hold you back. You will never know what job you could have, what you need to do to improve, or how badly you want something until you apply. Let's go!

> *You will never know what job you could have, what you need to do to improve, or how badly you want something until you apply. Let's go!*

Majalise's Story

GET AFTER IT!

As a teacher, I asked my principal when he had transitioned out of teaching. His response: "I got my administrator license in five, but you should probably wait ten." Really? Wait ten years. Why? Because I was a mother and wife? Because I loved the classroom and couldn't imagine not teaching? All I heard was that he could do it in five and I shouldn't.

I tackled that challenge head-on. After I had taught the required three years, I enrolled in an administrative program and completed my license just a few months before giving birth to our third child. I had no intention of using the license right away, because I loved the classroom and my position. My husband had just become the head football coach, we had wonderful friends, my new principal was amazing, and we were in the middle of remodeling a house. Who leaves all that? Well, we did. I left an amazing teaching situation so I could have more influence, take on more responsibility, and make decisions that would impact so much more than just my classroom.

When you are ready, know why you want to move to the new leadership position and why you want that exact position. If you can't honestly answer your "why," ask yourself why not. Leadership moves are not always easy. The higher up the ladder, the smaller the local peer network becomes. That is not to say it isn't good to make moves that will help set you up for your future career plans, but those moves can come with the personal loss of having close friends nearby to discuss your day or just unwind with.

Do the Research

You got an interview—high-five! (That never would've happened if you hadn't applied.) Now before the big day, do your research.

Even if you're putting your name in the hat for all the administrative openings in your local area, you need to show each interviewer that you understand why a particular position is special. They want to know that you truly want to be in their district serving their staff, students, and families. Before your interview, study up. Research the building, district, and community. Look into the culture of a building by browsing its website, social media accounts, and online handbooks. You might also chart out academic levels, including growth rates, especially for students who are historically marginalized or underserved. Finally, examine the staff and leadership turnover in the building and district. This is a telling piece of information that can help guide you during the interview process, as it can give insight into a culture and climate, as well as help you craft questions to ask during the interview process.

While an interviewer might not come straight out and ask you what you know about the district, you should plan on weaving that information into your responses, such as by referencing their district improvement plan or identifying specific strengths you would bring to the implementation of district goals and initiatives.

Craft an Elevator Pitch

Before you show up for your interview, come up with an elevator pitch, also known as an "elevator speech." This is a summary of who you are and why you want the job, which should be short and sweet—quick enough to give in an elevator before the doors open. The majority of all interviews, whether face-to-face or over the phone, start with the same prompt: "Tell us about yourself and why you are interested in the job." The good thing about a predictable question is you can prepare for it. As you craft your speech, here are a few things to keep in mind:

1. Consider why you want the job and why it is the perfect fit for you.
2. Craft your message based on the job description and your research on the building, district, or area in which you are interviewing.
3. Be passionate and specific about why you want this job.
4. Keep your response under two minutes and practice it with others.
5. In the interview, take a deep breath before responding to the question and speak slowly so your speech doesn't sound like a canned, artificial response.

―――――――――――――― *Rachael's Story* ――――――――――――

KNOW YOUR AUDIENCE

Every state, district, and building handles interviews differently. For some, you might start your day with a group interview along with all the other candidates, followed by a performance task of conducting an observation and debrief with a teacher on-site, along with a one-on-one meeting with the superintendent, and a final round of community questions and answers in the evening. Other locations might have you start with a building interview that consists of a panel made up of teachers, support staff, parents, and students, all of whom you have to get past to move on to the next round or to meet with the superintendent. Whatever the interview process looks like, know that understanding who is in the room with you and the role they play is vital to nailing that portion of the hiring process.

At the start of your interview, members of your interview committee will introduce themselves. Pay attention! Use what you know about your audience to guide your responses to interview questions. People also like to be honored for the work they have done, so make sure that you are able to include that within your responses, such as acknowledging their commitment to a specific success. For example, acknowledge the teachers on the committee for their hard work in lowering discipline rates or increasing student achievement in mathematics.

I was recently on a committee to hire a principal for another building. The group included teachers from the building as well as district office staff. As the interview process progressed, I noticed a significant difference in how the team was interpreting the candidates' responses. While I thought their answers were solid, the teachers had an entirely different take. The largest discrepancies occurred when candidates didn't explicitly say they would talk to a teacher first or collaborate with them.

As a principal, I thought this was a given. Surely everyone would ask for teacher input, thoughts, or guidance; there was no need to explicitly state it. The teachers, on the other hand, assumed the opposite. As you answer questions, consider who's on the committee and what assumptions they may make. Then respond in a way that makes sense for all points of view.

ACE YOUR INTERVIEW

Interviewing is an odd process. You have a narrow window of time to convince a committee of strangers that you belong within their ranks.

The good news: interviewing is a skill you can refine. The more you interview, the better you will do. I have mentored a number of new administrators who have hesitated to apply for a job because it is not their dream job; but there's value in interviewing for more than just your ideal position. Once you meet the committee, your view of a given job posting may change. The dream-job interview may reveal some facts that make that job less appealing, or the less ideal job might be better than it looked on paper. And besides, even if the less ideal jobs remain, well, less than ideal, you'll have gotten some interviews under your belt before you interview for your dream job.

The best interviews feel natural, like an interesting conversation. The worst ones feel awkward and stilted. Some major stumbles include long pauses while you think of an answer, saying you do not know how to answer a question, rambling, complaining at length about your last position or supervisor, or disclosing uncomfortable personal information and experiences (don't laugh—this happens!). Less obvious missteps include using excessive jargon and buzzwords, or asking questions you could answer with a quick skim of the website. A personal pet peeve is when a candidate writes down everyone's name as we make introductions; it takes forever and is something you can ask in your follow-up thank-you email (always send a thank-you email).

> *The best interviews feel natural, like an interesting conversation.*

How you appear in person and online also matters. I have never discounted a candidate for dressing too professionally, but the reverse can distract from your qualifications and make a committee hesitate. Be sure your online persona is professional, too. More and more people do a quick online search of potential candidates, so take a walk through your social media accounts and consider what an outsider might think.

Now that you know what not to do, let's talk about how to ace your interview. For starters, don't shy away from your humanity. Getting personal can work in your favor, even when you feel like you're at a disadvantage. For instance, if you're asked about a topic you have no direct experience in, draw from personal experience. People remember and respond more to personal stories and specifics far more than facts you have read or what you know as "the safe answer." It is okay to say "I haven't done that personally, but something similar is ___" and go from there.

Let your personality and your personal life shine through. You may be one of dozens of candidates, but a few interesting or unique stories can help you stand out. I interviewed a principal candidate who was a bull rider in college. Every time the committee debriefed, that stood out in our memory because it was just so unusual. I do not hesitate to mention my kids, dogs, hobbies, or interests. Chances are, something will resonate with one of the committee members.

Interview committees tend to feel very formal, and most members are fairly serious and overly professional at the start. I know an interview is going in the right direction when people start to "break character," interacting with me rather than simply asking questions. If someone asks a few follow-up questions, you didn't give enough information. If you have been talking for a while and people look checked out (doodling and checking their phone is not a good sign), rein it in. Facial expressions offer good clues. If you get smiles and handshakes at the end, you did something right.

It can be reassuring to remember that you leave an impression, whether or not you get the job. Three times when I didn't get a job, I received a follow-up call encouraging me to apply for other open positions because they liked what they saw in the interview. You may well be interviewing for a job that is already slotted for an internal candidate or an interim, and the interview is a formality. But you never know when you might be back at that table.

Katie Schweitzer

STRATEGIES:

- Even if you aren't 100 percent sure you want the job, accept the interview. It is great practice, and you never know what might happen.
- Be prepared. Research the school and district, and know how your skill set complements the work they are doing.
- Let your personality shine through. Smile, relax, and be yourself.
- Focus on sharing examples and specifics. If you don't have any for a particular question, draw on experiences with something similar you have done.
- When the interview process ends, write it all down. You will be able to use these notes to prepare for your next interview or to plan interviews for your own staff in the future.

Rachael's Story

STAND OUT FROM THE CROWD

As you prepare for an interview, identify a few key achievements that set you apart from others who may be interviewing for the position, such as facilitating professional learning communities or any state-wide leadership experience you have. When responding to an interviewer's questions, weave these points into your answer. For example, when asked about how you include student voice in decision-making, you can reference work you do at a statewide level to foster and create such a forum. If there isn't a natural place to mention your achievements when answering focused questions, highlight what sets you apart when asked if there's anything else you would like to tell the group.

When I was applying for my first principalship, I interviewed with a building across the state from where I lived. Facing a cramped conference room and a ton of intimidating people, I didn't feel the slightest bit confident. I forced myself to walk through the door and go through the interview process just for the opportunity to grow (I was sure I wouldn't land the job).

The first request was a simple "tell us about yourself." At the realization that I wasn't a principal or ready for the challenge, I panicked. I pictured myself walking out of the room and the awkwardness it would cause as I tried to crawl, squeeze, and leap over the four other people blocking the door. Instead of listening to the inner voice begging me to bolt for the door, I took a deep breath and answered the question. Sure, my voice quivered with nerves, but I shared about myself. As the interview progressed, I started to loosen up but still believed I wasn't ready for the job. Needless to say, I was completely shocked when the committee didn't agree with my self-reflection and I was hired.

Sometimes in interviews, we panic. We second-guess what we are doing, if we are worthy, or if we are even ready to take the next step in our careers. These are all legit feelings. If you find yourself in such a position, take a deep breath, plant your feet firmly on the floor, and keep going. You can do this!

INTERVIEW THEM TO ENSURE A GOOD FIT

I used to view the job hunt as a one-sided experience. I would study the company, memorize its vision and mission statements, identify organizational goals and pain points—and that was just the beginning of my research. My focus was on how I could convince the hiring manager and panel that I was worthy of their acceptance. I agonized over what to wear to the interview and how I would be perceived by the hiring team.

As I have grown, I've realized that this mindset had a negative impact on my sense of self-worth and belonging. (It also made me a nervous wreck during interviews.) It placed the employer's needs and ideas about me at the forefront, above my own. What I now understand is that the job search is a two-way transaction.

These days, I place myself at the center of the hiring process. I ask myself two major questions when considering a job: Is this organization or position a good fit for me and the trajectory of my career? Are the organization's mission and vision aligned with my own beliefs and values?

Sure, I still do my research on an organization and a position, but now I also come to the interview prepared with questions that get to the heart of my professional desires and interests. I also closely observe the behavior and mannerisms of the interview panel. This gives me an indication of the culture of the organization.

This change in mindset has strengthened my courage to step out of my comfort zone. The fear of applying for positions that may seem out of my reach has diminished. I have a grasp on the fact that I have a solid skill set that would bring value to any organization that truly aims to have a positive and meaningful impact on the lives of children and their families.

At the end of the day, I want to work for an organization that accepts me and my authenticity. When applying for positions, I seek out organizations that embrace diversity and value every member of their community. I want to work with people who are passionate about doing good work that benefits children, as well as the adults who work with them. I want to work in an organization with a culture built on honesty, trust, and integrity, and values innovation and creativity. When seeking new opportunities, I must position myself to serve these types of organizations by doing my homework and asking the questions that get to the heart of my desires.

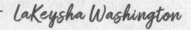

LaKeysha Washington

STRATEGIES:

- Think about the questions the panel asks. Are members focused on management, instruction, vision, or equity? Double-check that the panel's focus is your focus; if it's not, it might not be a good match.
- Consider how panel members respond to your responses. Make note of verbal and nonverbal cues, as they will help you determine if your beliefs align.
- If the panel asks at the end if you have any questions, pay attention to their answers.
- Gauge whether members of the panel appear to be on the same page and like each other. Panel interactions provide insight into the culture and climate of a district.
- Trust your judgment. If you do not feel good during the interview, acknowledge the need to continue looking to find the best fit.

Nix Negativity

As tempting as it may be to speak transparently and vulnerably with the interview panel, resist the urge to describe the nightmare job that has you looking elsewhere. You might be frustrated with a present employer or decision, but negative feelings shouldn't seep into your body language, tone of voice, or responses—even if you were wronged. Districts and buildings want to make a professional hire, so keep conversation positive, regardless of the circumstances for applying to a new position.

This does not mean you need to sugarcoat issues or concerns. A negative experience can be shared in a positive way. For example, maybe your leadership style and approach didn't align with your direct supervisor or the teacher's union, and therefore a change was needed. Negative interactions can sometimes serve as teaching moments, driving us to action. Through these experiences, we practice crucial conversation skills, enact change, and grow as leaders. In fact, sharing a negative experience and its outcome can help the panel see you as real and authentic, provided you frame it as an experience on your path to growing as a leader.

Give an Example

During your interview, avoid talking vaguely about how you might address a concern or situation. Instead, paint a clear picture of what the interview panel could expect from you in the position. You can do this by providing examples of how you handled a similar situation in your current role.

As you interview for positions of advancement, you may find you don't have experience to draw from. If you have watched a colleague handle a similar situation, you can use that as an example. For example, as an elementary teacher leader interviewing for a secondary administrative position, you may not have any experience with expulsions. However, your friend at the high school has, and you are able to talk about how that process looks from a teacher, administrative, student, and parent lens. Or, you pull an experience from your current job and explain how the lessons you learned might apply in the position you are interviewing for. When we were asked about how to support and grow teachers while interviewing for our first administrative jobs, we talked about leading building-wide professional development. While you might not have done this in the official administrative capacity, it doesn't mean you don't have comparable experiences. To prepare for the interview, spend some time watching and observing those above you and picking up leadership opportunities as they come your way. These experiences can be valuable for future interviews.

————————— *Rachael's Story* —————————

NEGOTIATING

Women are often uncomfortable negotiating, but it is one of the skills we perhaps need the most as we move into leadership. Instead of immediately accepting a job, put down the pen and negotiate like a pro. Employers expect you to negotiate, and men do it all the time. In fact, when you don't negotiate, you aren't valuing your true worth and skill set. You owe it to yourself—and the hard work you've done— to negotiate.

When my husband and I moved from one part of Oregon to another, we were approached by three different districts about working for them as building principals. We loved them all, so the choice came down to the contracts that each one was able to offer. We were very up-front with each district about what each of them was able to offer us in terms of the starting salary, all the components of each contract including fringe benefits such as health insurance caps, retirement benefits, and professional learning allocations, and how many total days each contract had, as some were year-round with vacation days while others had July off. As a team, we negotiated with each district and compared their best offer, weighing each against the things we needed and wanted in a location, such as retirement and health insurance caps.

This process was a first for me. In the past, I would have just taken what the district offered and been thankful to have a job. This experience taught me a key lesson: the salary range for a given position is much wider than you might think.

Usually the salary range is posted for the position when you apply for the job, such as $114,000 to $135,000 for the same job. If it is not posted, you can connect with your state association to find out what the average salary is for the position and location, or you can call and inquire with the district prior to applying. When negotiating a starting salary in a new job, always begin with a salary in the top of the range, regardless of your experience. Many times the salary schedule is based upon years of experience, and it's usually up to the superintendent to determine what counts as experience. For example, some districts will count the years you were an interim principal, while others won't. Other districts won't have a salary schedule for the number of years of experience you have, but instead a flat rate that all middle school, elementary principal, or other administrators are placed at. On the other hand, we have also known some folks with the same number of years of experience who were all paid different rates, even though they all worked within the same school district. Finding out that pay varies so dramatically was one of the most eye opening things I learned during my first few years.

Pay is something to consider as you look to move from one administrative position to another, as district pay can fluctuate. For example, in Oregon, principal pay can vary by $50,000 based upon the size and location of the district you are working in. If you are moving from an administrative position in one district to a similar position in a different district, you can use the knowledge of pay scales and comparable locations as a negotiating piece so you don't end up making less money. We have known leadership candidates, once they have been offered the job, to openly negotiate with superintendents using their daily rate or fringe benefits to help offset or minimize the potential for making less money in the long run.

During negotiations, determine your goal daily rate for the job you're applying to. Pay particularly close attention to the number of days you are contracted to work. When you move to the district office level, this knowledge will come in handy as you factor in additional days and hours. The goal is a rate that reflects an increase in work.

For example, imagine you are a building principal with a 225-day contract at a daily rate of $500—an annual total of $112,500. When negotiating a contract for a year-round district office job that is 290 days a year, you'd want to account for the extra days you'll be working at your new job before negotiating your annual salary, which could be an increase of twenty or more extra days a year. With the increase in days, you should have an increase of pay that is in alignment with your daily rate. While daily rates do vary, it is a good guide to make sure you aren't signing on to work more for less money.

Doing the math can help you spot when a job isn't financially worth your while. In the example above, the district may not be able to offer more than $112,500 per year. Perhaps your home and personal life won't accommodate your working more days for the same or less money. Or maybe the position provides you an opportunity to lead at the next level, making the pay cut worth it. These are all things to consider during the negotiation process.

Still nervous about asking for greater compensation? The worst they can say is no, and then you'll sign the contract that was initially offered.

Consider Your Needs

Negotiating isn't just about your pay rate. It's also a time to ask for what you need. We had a mentor who often talked about knowing your "asks" when considering a new position. What will you need in order to be successful at your new job? Our mentor always brought her own administrative assistant, and they traveled as a team as she moved from building to building and district to district.

Perhaps you need certain teachers to move with you to a new building in order to make the changes your superintendent wants. Or maybe you need transitional days added as you plan and prepare for the new job. As you work through your initial contract negotiation, determine who or what you need. Then ask for it.

As you consider your needs, we encourage you to calculate additional days that you might need to help create a seamless transition to this new job. Would five extra days help so that you can meet with existing staff to hear about what is working or what is not? You might also want to find out what memberships to professional organizations are covered within your compensation package. Or check on professional development funding or continuing education allocations so you can continue learning or growing. Don't forget to ask about and research your retirement account options. Is there an opportunity to contribute to a retirement account, separate from what the state offers? Finally, don't forget to ground your ask in your "why."

Some of our closest women colleagues balk at the idea of asking for what they need, assuming they'll look too confident. That might be the case, but only if you don't ask properly.

Much of negotiation connects back to communication. Ask for what you need, and provide your rationale. Often, the person who makes the decision regarding your contract and compensation package is not fully up to speed on the incredible work you have done. They are looking to you to be confident in your proposal and point of view. If you negotiate in person, keep your body language, speech, facial expressions, and overall enthusiasm for the job positive.

Worst-Case Scenario

As you refine your negotiation skills and work to overcome uncomfortable self-doubt, reflect on the best and worst things that could happen if you negotiate.

The best outcome is that you are paid at a rate that is on par with your colleagues of different demographic groups. You are compensated for your knowledge and the work you are doing at a level that is comfortable and appropriate to you.

In the worst-case scenario, you end up right where you started, with the same pay rate and compensation plan you were initially offered. You still have the job offer and can determine if the pay is acceptable to you. If it isn't, you can walk away.

We know negotiating doesn't come easy. We don't like to talk about ourselves and tend to undervalue our work and our advancements. Like it or not, you owe it to yourself to fight for what you deserve. What do you have to lose?

CHART YOUR PATH

⚓ What are the key attributes you are looking for in a school, district, and/or community that you will serve as a leader?

⚓ The hiring process can be long and complex. What aspects make you most nervous and excited? Who can help guide you through the process?

Chapter 5

Supporting Women Leaders

I t is time to start breaking through the walls, glass ceilings, and gender roles that exist in education. Alone, this fight is difficult. Working against one another, the task is practically impossible.

It can be tempting to assume that there are a limited number of leadership roles for women. After all, fewer women fill leadership positions than men. Don't fall for this false belief. Any position can be filled by a female leader; there's no limit to how many women can lead. We need to shift away from competing with other women. In a 2020 article in *Harvard Business Review* devoted to stopping female rivalry, CEO, author, and executive coach Mikaela Kinder said, "If a woman wants to get ahead, the better course is to champion women around her, resulting in more opportunities and increased success for all."

Once in a leadership role, it is imperative we work to support and lift up other women. Think about the possibilities if all women leaders in education supported other women. An army of female leaders would pave the way for other women to follow, and the leadership opportunities and positions would be endless.

> *Think about the possibilities if all women leaders in education supported other women.*

IT STARTS AT AN EARLY AGE

I heard recently that Mrs. Hampton moved away. A well-loved teacher, Mrs. Hampton had taught at our elementary school forever, then retired and worked at the local Walmart. She was a member of a sorority that each year sponsored the community penny drive for St. Jude's Hospital. Mrs. Hampton was a cheerful lady who could always be found supporting, assisting, and nurturing. When I heard she had moved away, I recalled a memory that had been deeply buried for such a long time.

"Don't be afraid, Julie," Mrs. Hampton said. She coaxed me into the classroom. Now that I think about it, she might have actually given me a little scoot. "Go right up to the table. Just get in there and you will see who needs the help." "How will I know?" I asked. "Oh, you will know!" Mrs. Hampton laughed. "Their eyes could be where their ears go. Their nose may be where their chin belongs. They might even be missing their mouths!"

As a high school freshman, I had been selected to spend the day shadowing Mrs. Hampton in her elementary classroom. I had never really been around small children. I was quiet, shy, and reluctant. But there I was, shadowing to pursue my interest in becoming a teacher. I approached the table of children, who were armed with scissors and paste. And Mrs. Hampton was right! I instinctively knew what to do. Of course, it isn't difficult to determine who needs help when small children are pasting faces together, but nonetheless, it felt right. That day, Mrs. Hampton opened my eyes to the world of teaching, which I would later choose as my career path.

As community leaders, it is crucial for us to provide young women opportunities to explore career paths and opportunities for leadership. Partnerships with teachers in my local district have allowed my school to mentor students who have an interest in becoming educators. Many refer to it as "the teacher pipeline" or the answer to the teacher shortage. We call it "growing teachers."

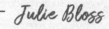
— *Julie Bloss*

STRATEGIES:

- Choose a project day when students and the teacher will need extra "hands on deck" to assist. Giving students a task to assist with helps them become involved and engaged.
- Pair a shy or reluctant leader (one who may need a little scoot) with a partner to assist. Once acclimated, their reluctance may simply melt away. You just might see leadership rise to the occasion!
- Sit down with student leaders before volunteering so that everyone is aware ahead of time what the day or task will look like. And if you aren't available, lean on another leader to help. Leadership opportunities grow leadership in others!

Majalise's Story

YOU CAN'T KEEP US APART

My first year of teaching, I took over a position for a well-loved teacher who had been reassigned to advanced students elsewhere in the building. I was jealous to say the least.

The first few months were terrible. Short of a quick rundown on how to run the class, I had no guidance. The principal told me the teacher who had recently left the position wouldn't help me. Yet staff said I was irrational for not reaching out to her because we were so much alike.

As fate would have it, our classes ended up on a field trip together, and we had to work with each other. Andrea was inspiring—and had been under the impression I didn't want her help in the classroom. (Yes, the same principal had led her to believe that.) I left the trip with a life-long friend and mentor.

The following year, she became my supervisor, and her candid communication and feedback led to my leadership growth. Even now, she gets emergency text messages from me, and before she retired, I had the chance to give her my opinion on some things as well. She taught me to be authentic and transparent while showing grace when our leader tried to intentionally keep two strong women apart.

The stakes are high and we need to connect and communicate with others in order to lead well and make a difference in education. We encourage you to get to know everyone you work with, especially other women who have information or skills that could help you do your job better, and therefore better serve students. Finally, reach out to those in the building or district who teach the same subject or grade level as you, have been on the teams you now lead, or have experience in sociopolitical situations that might be new to you in your position. Their advice and insight will be valuable, and it all starts with connection.

IT'S NOT A COMPETITION

When it comes to educational leadership, women are the minority. Too many women hear this fact and adopt the mentality that it's a fight to the top. But we don't need to step on one another to reach our goals. Together, we have more power. Together, we can all win.

In my tenure, I have only worked under female leaders. While I wish each experience had been positive, I'll be honest: they weren't.

Once, after sharing my goals with a leader, our relationship soured. I was no longer her thought partner. From that point on, she questioned every decision I made. And I had no idea why. That experience scarred me for a long time. It became difficult to talk about it in conversations, and when probed about that job in interviews, I couldn't speak about the experience without feeling defeated.

It took a lot of reflection and strategic relationship-building to move on from that bad experience. That leader had been my mentor; I'd wanted her to be proud of me, to see me as her protégé. It wasn't until much later I learned the reason behind our rift: She had been afraid of how far my goals would take me. But I never wanted her position. I just wanted to learn as much as I could from her.

Let's just say it: There are not a limited number of positions that are reserved for women in leadership. There is not a fixed number of "female slots." We need to stop being jealous, as we each have the potential and ability to reach these heights of educational leadership. Instead of judging and competing with others, stop and reflect. When you do this to others, what does it say about you as a person and as a leader? If we truly want women to succeed within educational leadership, we need to stop competing and instead put our hand out to help.

—  Ryan Daniel

STRATEGIES:

- Be proud of the accomplishments of other women.
- Instead of viewing others as competition, realize that their work is helping pave the way for all women.

- Applaud and celebrate the work of women at all levels of educational leadership.
- If you are in a leadership position, help mentor other women leaders.

———————————— *Majalise's Story* ————————————

EXTERNAL JUDGEMENT HAPPENS

A hard truth of leadership we both have experienced is that not everybody likes or agrees with us. As a leader, you may desperately want to control how others respond to and treat you. The fact is, there will be people out there who won't stop publicly scrutinizing you until all of your staff, community, and stakeholders are in agreement with your leadership and decisions.

We have had to get comfortable with being judged and doubted. It comes with success. Instead of focusing on others' opinions of us, we have let the hate, doubt, and judgment fuel our chase for greatness. Strong women leaders shake off the criticism and keep moving.

Strong women leaders shake off the criticism and keep moving.

While mentoring an aspiring leader recently, she asked how to handle personal versus professional decision-making in a small town. The key is being able to separate the procedural decision-making and the personal connections.

There are times people don't agree with a policy or a procedure and can completely dislike the outcome and decision. It does not mean they dislike the woman who delivered that decision. It doesn't mean the woman who delivered it won't need to take a moment to emotionally come to terms with the outcome. With that being said, the leader has to be the first person to accept the outcome.

There was a time I suspended a student based on policy. The parent, a friend, was very upset with the decision and wanted to file a complaint. Most leaders don't like to know complaints are being filed against them, but it can happen. I calmly said, "If you are filing a complaint against this policy that I am enforcing, please call this number to start the complaint process. If you are filing the complaint against me for how I am handling the policy, please call my direct supervisor." That separation did not help the parent, my friend, but it did help me emotionally separate the situation. This response ended up being a strategy I would use in the future when someone was upset, so that I could remember it wasn't always about me.

In the same vein, don't let yourself judge others. Whether you are thinking about how a woman looks when she is presenting or lashing out in jealousy after learning she has written another book, judgment of others happens all the time, in our heads and out loud. Another woman's personal time and leadership style are not something you can control.

Judgment of others comes from personal insecurities and experiences. When you find yourself in a moment of judgment, reflect on your own dreams instead. Energy spent moving forward is the best energy to expend.

Majalise's Story

WHAT WORKED FOR YOU MAY NOT WORK FOR OTHERS

When I was a teacher, two of my four children were born during the school year. I was incredibly blessed to have an amazing retired teacher cover my maternity leave. We collaborated on the standards to be covered, while he planned and graded the work. I reviewed student work on Sunday nights and still felt like I knew my students. This system was perfect: I was able to stay home with my newborn, I could engage with work I was passionate about, and my anxiety stayed down. Our family had found the perfect balance.

Three years later, my first full year as building principal kicked off with the birth of my fourth child. My husband and I decided to work half days and pass our baby off in the middle of the day. When I needed to be at the school for a full day, my baby was in my front-pack baby carrier. Could the administrative substitute and assistant principal have handled the building without me? Absolutely. But I needed the professional connection. I was lucky to work for a district that allowed me to take my baby to work when I wasn't responsible for supervising students or leading meetings. Once again, our family had found a balance that worked for us emotionally and professionally.

It worked so well that I assumed, rather unfairly, that teachers would want to be part of the ongoing conversation around their classrooms and student progress while they were on maternity leave. While I took very little personal time, I assumed the same would be true for others. As you may have guessed, I was wrong.

For me, conversations about maternity leave were very difficult to have the first few times a teacher had a baby. How a mother handles pregnancy, birth, and raising kids can be a sensitive topic and is deeply personal. I had to own up: I couldn't wrap my head around the fact that some women's view of maternity leave left work behind. Shifting my viewpoint took collaboration with the expecting mothers and understanding their needs. As leaders, we must support working mothers without judging them or making them feel guilty for a decision that differs from ours.

It is important for women to remember that what worked for them may not work for other women in the workplace. This may be as complex as navigating maternity leave, or as simple as finding coverage to take a child to the dentist. We have also seen it come up when there have been gender expectations at potlucks or bake days at work. Things like workplace bridal or baby showers, and even birthday celebrations, may be something some women want and not others. It is important to remember that all staff have a voice and needs in and out of the workplace and to not superimpose what worked for us in our leadership process.

─────────────── *Majalise's Story* ───────────────

SHE'S GOT YOUR BACK

Early in my career, I attended a pretty intense administrative meeting about school improvement. The laundry list of ways our building was unsuccessful overwhelmed me. I felt like I needed to understand talented and gifted education, Title I budgeting, instructional reading support, English language learner program implementation, the hiring and evaluation process, mental health for students, special education instruction, and individualized education plans, all while increasing attendance rates and test scores. I couldn't possibly be an expert in everything all at once. I listed all of those items for the group, then asked for guidance on prioritizing them in my role as the building principal. My "please" was met with frustration and negativity from my supervisor (I'll admit: my delivery was poor). As I fought back anger and tears, my coworkers remained silent.

Later, at lunch, a few colleagues said they were sorry it had happened and that they hadn't spoken up. I didn't need a sorry, I told them. I needed them to have my back when I asked a question we had all raised in side conversations. I took the verbal risk and wanted support.

The issue was, I never asked them to support me, and I hadn't told them I would say anything. They weren't prepared for me to question district leadership, either. When we step out on our own to make a statement, we might not get support right away. If what I wanted was immediate support, I should have provided my colleagues with the opportunity to process prior to raising the questions.

When a woman steps up to make a statement on which we agree, even if we aren't ready, we must find the strength to support her. If you agree, voice your support or agreement, even if it is not popular or comfortable at the moment. We also encourage women to share ideas, even if they are outside the box. These are vulnerable times, so when someone steps out and shares what they need, support them and don't undercut them by trying to be better or to compete. Finally, if you see a fellow woman leader doing something awesome, help share the idea and celebrate it. Whether you do this in a virtual meeting, at the boardroom table, or on social media, we encourage you to have each other's backs.

IT'S ABOUT THE PEOPLE

I heard the ping on my cell phone. It was Wednesday morning and I was humming along, literally and figuratively. I checked off a couple of things on my to-do list and even finished some of those "I know you're busy, but do you have a minute" sessions. I could hear faculty and staff excitedly chatting as they waited for students and families to pick up their devices at the curbside meet and greet. It was going to be another good day. Even though I hesitated to check the text message because my inbox was already overflowing, I knew that I couldn't put it off. As I reached for my phone, I thought about being accessible and having an open door policy versus being available 24-7. Other principals will say that it is the nature of the job. But is it really? I reached for my phone and there was a text from my mentor, Catherine. Surprised? Absolutely.

I leaned back and reread her message several times. Her message was so timely and full of care. Then the tears came. The heartfelt, gut-wrenching, cathartic sobs that caused me to double over. I had never cried at work, let alone sobbed. But at that moment, I hadn't a thought about what people might think. I didn't think it was unprofessional. I didn't worry about whether people would see me as less effective because I was crying. Her message to me was affirming and acknowledged that the leadership decisions I made, and the way I communicated, were right for my school. And coming from my mentor, it was that much more meaningful. As the sole administrator on my campus, I wonder about situations and decisions constantly. Catherine's message, I felt it in my core. She thanked me for remaining positive and said that she knew I would continue to guide my school. "I know you are wrapping your arms around everyone, and that is so important now."

More so now than ever, I know that school leadership is about people: caring for and caring about them. When I began this adventure, I had another mentor, Ted. We would walk the campus, and he would talk with me about things ranging from the broken window theory to changes in correctional facilities. But the thread, throughout our conversations, was to make sure that my decision-making remains people-centered, addresses needs, and is true to myself, my style.

— *Laurie Luczak*

STRATEGIES:

- It's easy to get bogged down in the daily grind of our work. Remember to put people first.
- Relationships, relationships, relationships.
- Reach out to those you support and send an encouraging word.

— *Majalise's Story* —

THE POWER OF THE MENTOR

A strong group of supporters is essential for leaders. But to really succeed, you need a mentor. Someone to help guide you on your leadership journey, answer questions, connect you with resources, be a listening ear, and celebrate your successes with you. However, mentors also play a critical role in providing regular and consistent feedback as they help you see blind spots and reflect on your practice. This is something we can't do alone. Sometimes mentors are assigned, while other times they are found organically, through professional networks or social connections. Mentors provide a safe and consistent space for mentees to grow, learn, and process, all while being vulnerable in their leadership development.

As a teacher and now as an administrator, I have a mentor who I look to for advice and guidance. He didn't ask to be a mentor, and I didn't seek him out. And, yes, my mentor is a man. A leadership mentor's gender doesn't matter. His or her skill set, integrity, and ability to ask questions and provide feedback does.

When I was a teacher, I was always asking questions of Ralph, my principal. He knew I wanted to be a leader and that my fiery spirit had a tendency to get in the way of my message. Not once did Ralph try to dissuade me from pushing for what is right, but he did talk to me about my delivery and advised I choose the right battles. For example, he taught me to separate the policy or situation from the individuals involved.

Mentors teach more than the ins and outs of a given position. They teach us about ourselves and how integrity fits into the leadership equation. I can call Ralph anytime and he will help me weigh decisions, offering options I might not even see. But first he'll ask how my family is. Mentors do that, too. They care about the whole person, and they know that leaders are people with real emotions and stress.

THE DIFFERENCE A MENTOR MAKES

Looking back on my thirty-year career as a school leader, there are many highlights: serving as an administrator at all levels (high school, middle school, and elementary); learning from highly qualified, dedicated educators; watching students blossom into contributing members of society and welcoming their children into my elementary school as the next generation of learners; enjoying the role of servant-leader contributing to our school community; and working at the local, state, and national levels to better our chosen profession. None of this would have been possible without the guidance and support of mentors along the way.

One of my first mentors was Connie Honaker, the principal of Highland High School in Gilbert, Arizona. Highland was a brand-new school, and with 4,200 students, it was the largest comprehensive high school in the state. That September, I was the last administrator hired, with an extensive list of responsibilities. I was unsure how I would be successful in accomplishing all that was asked of me, so I asked my principal to be my mentor.

Connie also opened my eyes to the many benefits of active membership and participation in state and national organizations, such as National Association of Elementary School Principals, National Association of Secondary School Principals, Association for Supervision and Curriculum Development, and Arizona School Administrators. Under her leadership, I not only survived my first year as a high school assistant principal, I thrived. I knew school administration would be my lifelong career thanks to her guidance and friendship. Connie has since retired but remains a good friend.

I've since moved to a principalship at an elementary school, where I've mentored several new administrators in the district. Understanding the importance of having a good mentor, I also sought mentorship from a principal with federal programs knowledge that I did not possess. I asked the principal of another elementary school to mentor me with Title I requirements. Even though she was younger than I was and less experienced overall, she had the expertise that I desperately needed in order to remain successful in leading a Title I school. We arranged a time to meet so she could share knowledge and experience that my school community and I greatly needed. She was so kind and patient with me as she answered my many questions, sometimes the same one over and over.

No matter where I've been at in my career, guidance and support from a mentor have proven invaluable. If I am a good leader, it's only because I surrounded myself with great leaders.

———————————————————— *Robyn Hansen*

STRATEGIES:

- Find or act as a mentor to others.
- Don't let age limit you on who you view as a mentor in your personal or professional career.
- Actively join your state and national associations.
- Connect with others in your district and state; you never know who might end up serving as a mentor for you.

Where the Mentors Are

Mentors are everywhere you look. They are in your building as teacher-leaders, they are at the district office, and they are in nearby districts. Mentors can even be found on social media or across the nation from you. Mentors know no boundaries; you just have to keep your eyes peeled. While official mentor programs exist, we have both benefited from finding unofficial mentors along the way. These relationships tend to be more authentic and a better fit for our personalities. For us, they started with us reaching out to our respective mentors to ask for some input, guidance, or thoughts on something we were struggling with. From there, we kept the conversation going as the weeks, months, and years went on. Over time, the conversations have deepened along with our mentor/mentee relationships. On the flip side, your building or district will sometimes assign you a mentor, but not always. It often comes down to funding, systems and structures the building or district has in place, and the priority of supporting leaders. Having both formal (assigned to you) and informal mentors will provide you with diverse insight and perspective.

So absolutely work with your formal mentor, but also establish a wide network of people who can help you. Look to family members, colleagues, members of associations you belong to, and friends. Think about how you are connecting with them and seeking input.

As you seek out and develop your network of mentors, keep a special eye out for those whose careers are more advanced than yours. We have found that we frequently interact more with others who have the same type of job. For example, we've seen female teachers mostly interact with female teachers, and female principals primarily interact with female principals. As women looking to move up in leadership ranks, we have come to realize our interactions with those above us may be limiting and require us to reach outside of our building or district to find mentors whose experience is more aligned with our career position or goals. For instance, there is often only one assistant principal in a building, so connecting with another female assistant principal may require reaching out through professional organizations for a more experienced mentor for support. Mentors also come in all genders, roles, and avenues of education, so you may find a leader in a different profession who has strengths in personal growth areas.

Finally, it may be that more than one mentor is needed. An assigned mentor at work may or may not be an authentic mentor, and as a leader, you might need both. A true mentor-mentee relationship is personal and authentic, while the work-assigned mentor may be able to support you in system and logistical requirements, like how to make a purchase through their requisition process or use the student management system. It is okay to realize your mentor might not be one-size-fits-all. While we would never want to suggest you clog your calendar with mentor-mentee meetings, we do want you to know that mentors are out there, willing and waiting to support you. You just have to ask.

──────────── *Majalise's Story* ────────────

ENLISTING HELP

When connecting with other women at conferences, our conversations have often included talking about our full calendars. Knowing this about other female leaders, it can be hard to make the ask when it is time to find a mentor. However, it is important to remember that you will never know if someone has time to mentor you until you ask. In our experience, women who are willing to sit and talk over coffee or a drink at a conference are just as willing to answer text messages or a phone call when a situation arises that needs a mentor's support. I am currently a mentor for a woman outside the education field. When she called to ask me, she was so nervous to ask for time out of my schedule. I was so proud of her for taking the brave step in asking for a mentor to support her growth. I said yes before she even finished asking. The amazing part is that I'm learning just as much or more in this relationship.

─────────────────────────────────────

WHAT MAKES A MENTOR

When I was younger, I loved teachers and coaches who would tout my greatness. I never realized how much of a disservice they were doing to me. The administrators who've had the greatest impact on me cared enough to find my areas of weakness, point them out to me, and push me to really develop and defend my thinking.

Noting your shortcomings, however, is only half of the game. Great mentors support and encourage you in your growth and will be with you every step of the way. Through this nurturing, constructive feedback, you can prove your worth by taking what your mentors say to heart while passionately and actively pursuing change.

Phenomenal mentors will not only help you find areas to improve upon, but they will also highlight the strengths and gifts you already possess. Nothing feels better than someone you admire pointing out what makes you unique. This, in turn, reinforces your belief in yourself. It is after this intensive coaching that your in-district mentor should begin to empower you to take risks and be the best educator you can be.

I am so fortunate that I have had amazing mentors who have helped me grow into the strong female educator I am today. Because of these inspiring people, I now feel confident in implementing changes on campus that champion students in all of their pursuits. One day, I hope to be fortunate enough to help another aspiring administrator grow into a capable leader.

Chloe Minch

STRATEGIES:

- A mentor's job is to help you identify weaknesses and highlight your strengths. It is important that you be in a place to accept both forms of feedback.
- When your mentor encourages you to take risks, take advantage of their support to develop your leadership skills.
- Pay it forward. When you are ready, make time to mentor other women who are looking to lead. We need each other to increase diversity and raise female voices.

Majalise's Story

SO YOU WANT TO BE A MENTOR

As you advance in your career, you may choose to share your knowledge and experience with up-and-coming women leaders by being a mentor. Because I had such a great mentor, you'd think I would be a natural at the mentorship thing. You'd be wrong.

Two weeks after I started my first high school principal position, I hired two brand-new assistant principals. Unfortunately, I started out unprepared and was a terrible mentor. In one particularly negative interaction, my assistant principal asked me a question, and I completely snapped at her. Her eyes filled with tears, and she said she had no idea I felt that way. Here was a first-year assistant, working tirelessly with a clueless first-year principal, and the only possible mentor in the room was rude.

While my assistant principal didn't ask me to be her mentor, she wanted to be a strong leader and I was her support on that path. Looking back, I see she was chasing feedback that I was failing to give. I called my supervisor after the incident to tell him how terrible I had been and to figure out what I needed to do better. My supervisor, another mentor who still gets calls from me, gave me very practical advice about how to communicate and ask questions. He even met with our team to outline leadership growth plans so I could support my mentees or find support elsewhere to help them grow.

Mentors don't always have supervisory authority over their mentees. But supervisors can always be mentors, and this should be one of our main goals. When we build up the organization and the leaders within it, we all win.

It is also important to remember that being a mentor can be tricky at times. Understanding your mentor/mentee relationship on a formal or informal level is important. For starters, don't assume someone wants a mentor, or that they don't already consider you to be their mentor. We encourage you to explicitly talk about the mentor/mentee relationship, such as the frequency with which you will connect and how you will do so, whether over the phone, in person for coffee, or on a Zoom call. Relationships and trust are crucial in developing a working partnership for growth, so ask questions. What does your mentee want to grow? Support their career path plan by reading the situation and asking how you can support them.

If your mentorship is formal, don't expect to do it perfectly without guidance or training. As I learned, there are specific ways to coach and mentor aspiring or beginning administrators. Rely on your own mentor to support you in your new role as a mentor, and attend professional development training to learn important mentoring skills. *Blended Coaching* by Gary Bloom, Claire Castagna, Ellen Moir, and Betsy Warren is an excellent resource we recommend to support a more formal mentor process for principals.

Rachael's Story

LEARN FROM YOUR PEERS

Like many of you, I am a self-professed lifelong learner. While having mentors has been vital to my growth, so has the use of a peer coach who has similar leadership responsibilities and shared experiences.

Over the years, I have enlisted principals and other instructional leaders in my building to provide coaching and feedback when I can't talk to my mentor. Most recently I have been working on my facial expressions and nonverbal cues when talking with someone. These are easy to manage when the conversation is light and positive; however, you can read displeasure all over my face when I'm not happy. (I am not good at playing poker for this exact reason.)

I asked for help and feedback, and my Title I teacher offered to watch my facial expressions during a meeting. As my colleagues and I worked through the topic at hand, there were bumpy and smooth parts of the conversation. After the meeting, the teacher provided some perspective and feedback about how it went, noting my face had started tightening a few times, but I quickly caught myself and relaxed. This feedback helped me in future meetings, because I knew exactly what to focus on improving.

If you are looking to add another layer of support and growth through the use of a peer coach, we encourage you to make sure they are trustworthy. Confidentiality is a must, and following a formalized process to solicit coaching from them is incredibly helpful. Strategies found in Elena Aguilar's *The Art of Coaching: Effective Strategies for School Transformation* are extremely helpful when setting up coaching systems. As you set up the process, you will want to ensure your coach is comfortable with the area of development and is able to help. Therefore, you will want to stick to the area of focus that you decide on. This will help keep things positive and free from surprises.

CHART YOUR PATH

⚓ Have you ever found yourself in a negative competition with another female leader? If so, how was it resolved? If not, what steps can you take to ensure you are in a position of lifting other women up and not competitively holding them back?

⚓ In what ways can you mentor other women leaders? Who are women you could reach out to for mentorship, and whom could you spend time mentoring in turn?

Chapter 6

Networking

There are multiple ways to learn about new jobs, such as looking at job postings or growing professionally through reading books, but the power of networking can check all the boxes when it comes to job searches, recruitment, career advancement, professional growth, and problem-solving. Having a group of women you can reach out to in your own district, state, or using a virtual professional learning network (PLN) on platforms like Facebook or Twitter allows you to grow with like-minded women in a safe and inspiring way. For example, you never know when that leader you met in a Twitter chat may be able to connect you with someone to help your culinary teacher increase cultural diversity text in her classroom.

Majalise's Story

BUILD RELATIONSHIPS, FURTHER YOUR CAREER

When I first became a high school principal, I immediately knew I needed to lean on my professional organization, Coalition of Oregon School Administrators (COSA). The organization provides professional learning, networking, administrator socials, and group activities at national conferences. They even lead a monthly Zoom meeting just for female superintendents in the state. In fact, Rachael and I met through COSA. Overall, this network has been valuable for leaders looking to learn more about other districts and positions that are open. It is one thing to see a job posting and check out a website, visit a school, and read about a community. It is another thing to be able to have a network of leaders to call to tell you more about their experience with the district's diversity and inclusion practices, academic achievement, and staff culture and climate. A network allows you to ask hard questions before the interview, like how accepting this district or community will be of a female leader and what challenges a new female leader will face. And your network can also help ask questions for you and guide you in your professional growth processes to advance your career based on district needs.

Find Your People

To reap the full benefits of networking, think beyond the average professional relationship. Aim to maintain relationships with people who lift you up, not tear you down.

A friend of ours, Karen Ramirez, who is an elementary principal, told us about a networking event that doubles as an impromptu support group. There, she and other female elementary principals work together to plan and discuss how to make things work for their buildings. "This group has made the work lighter," she says. "It's more fun and doable since we don't have any vice principals and we are in silos within our buildings." It is her belief that we are stronger together, that we make better decisions when we can collaborate with our colleagues and support one another.

Consider your professional network and those you spend the most time with. Are they lifting you up or holding you down? By telling you that you can't balance coaching principals or presenting on topics you are passionate about while leading a building, your fellow principals may be cutting off your ambitions before you learn what you're capable of. On the flip side, if your peer group encourages you to find ways to balance leadership with being a present parent, they're supporting you in your career goals.

Who you surround yourself with truly impacts your goals and aspirations. When networking, build relationships with people who will lift you up, challenge you, and encourage you and your wild and crazy dreams. You decide who you want to spend time with. If every person (or even just one person) around you is negative, it's time for a change. That's where networking comes in.

> *Who you surround yourself with truly impacts your goals and aspirations.*

— *Rachael's Story* —

CONNECT WITH COLLEAGUES

During my first year as a principal, I noticed all of the secondary principals and vice principals would go out for a beverage after administrative meetings. As a middle school principal, I was often invited. The first two times my colleagues asked me to join, I turned them down. I thought it would be awkward—I was one of only two women principals and the only one they invited that night. After the third invite, I finally accepted. Once again, I would be the only female leader.

Looking back, this decision was probably one of the best I made. That happy hour taught me that much of the planning, preparation, and debriefing conversations that happened in leadership didn't always occur in the meeting. Instead, they took place off campus and during off hours. I also realized networking happened during social time. As my relationships and connections improved, the extent to which my colleagues trusted and listened to me during administrative meetings increased significantly once they knew and respected me as a person versus as a random colleague.

We should point out that men and women create relationships differently. Women often connect by talking, while men do so by doing things together, like golf. Educational leadership is a male dominated field, so make an effort to think creatively about your relationships. You're not just building relationships with other female leaders, but with the men, too.

So, how exactly do you network with colleagues? For starters, join them at social events. This is a great way to start your relationship-building, and these connections will follow you into the workplace. The more you go out of your way to know your coworkers, the more the level of your connections will increase. So, if you are invited to something after hours, you should say yes and show up!

Finding support outside of your district is vital to success, as it provides alternative ways of thinking and more global advice. These people don't know the personalities and politics that occur within your department, office, building, or district. Outside supports are often perfect for career planning, advice, and guidance during tough times at work.

Finding support outside of your district is vital to success.

There are many ways to find support outside of your district. Over the years, we have had success with networking events, social media networking, association conferences, and workshops, or using our existing networks to meet other like-minded professionals.

Networking Online

Networking may seem like a great strategy for professional growth and external support, but for a more introverted woman, it may seem overwhelming to walk up to others during a social networking event held at a conference. In fact, we know that chatting up a vendor for a free drink ticket at the social is not for everyone. It also may not be possible to get to conferences or take extended time when there on-site to meet and greet others face-to-face. For women in this position, connecting on social media platforms provides a more flexible opportunity to network with leaders across the country.

In today's world of high-speed internet, women are able to connect with leaders like never before. Seek out social media connections to meet women educational leaders from all over the country. Twitter chats like #LeadLAP, led by Beth Houf and Shelley Burgess, authors of *Lead Like a Pirate*, and #GritCrewEdu, led by Traci Browder and Dawn Harris, connect leaders across the country for forty-five-minute Twitter chats where users follow the hashtags #LeadLAP or #GritCrewEdu and join other leaders to answer five or six questions posed to the group. This virtual "chat" allows for leaders to connect and problem-solve with other leaders on current issues in instruction, diversity and inclusion, building culture, and educational leadership. Facebook groups like Leading While Female also allow for group users to pose questions and are another way for women to find one another, join in on book studies, and to grow professionally without leaving their home or school.

Make the Most of Your Contacts

Networking doesn't end with relationship building. When it comes time to move into your next position, shift from building and fostering relationships to leveraging them—that is, using them to support your career goals. Leveraging relationships is a must in order to conquer new heights of educational leadership.

How does this help you advance your career? Think about it this way: People often trust the judgement of those they like and have a relationship with. If your supervisor adores you and has a great working relationship with the person who's interviewing you for a new job, mention the connection in the interview (but ask your supervisor for permission first). Or if a friend has an established relationship with someone you'd like to meet, ask if they would be willing to connect the two of you. You would be surprised at how often the response is yes.

You might also think about connecting people who have similar interests and passions within education. This is big. If you help connect people, other people will help connect you. So if one of your contacts is looking to fill a position and another is job hunting and perfect for the role, introduce them. If a colleague would be a great keynote speaker for an upcoming conference that one of your connections organizes, send an introductory email.

As you assist your network, consider who you're helping. It is vital to have a diverse group of professional connections so your support doesn't add to in-group favoritism, which is one of the main contributing factors to the relevant disadvantages of Black Americans and other underrepresented groups, according to the book *Blindspot: Hidden Biases of Good People* by Mahzarin R. Banaji and Anthony G. Greenwald.

CHART YOUR PATH

⚓ Who is in your in-building, in-district, in-state, and online networks?

⚓ How can you utilize the power of the internet to connect with leaders who may have different perspectives or experiences in education and leadership than you see on a day-to-day basis?

Chapter 7

Risk Taking

In order to reach their goals, leaders have to be comfortable taking risks. That can be a challenge—after all, risks come with the possibility of failure. We have found ourselves trying to be people-pleasers, and we know we aren't alone. We often believe pleasing others comes from a drive to be perfect and not make mistakes. So we take small, safe risks. Or we practice new skills, speech delivery, or presentation techniques in private to ensure we have success and are confident when in front of others. However, failure is unavoidable. We will fall, but we have to get back up while not apologizing and while learning from our mistakes.

Rethink Perfect

Many women feel that the relentless drive for perfection may be, in part, a product of their upbringing. In her book *Brave Not Perfect*, author Reshma Saujani shares that well-meaning parents and educators often guide girls to activities and endeavors they will be good at instead of encouraging them to embrace ones that might provide a struggle or even failure. For instance, when young children, especially girls, want to sing or dance in a school talent show, they may be discouraged by those closest to them, who are trying to save them from an adult's fear of embarrassment. This gentle guiding follows girls into adulthood and forms the foundation for many women's struggles with perfectionism.

The belief in the value of perfection impacts women from all walks of life. (Consider how many times you've heard a woman say she's a perfectionist and likes to do her job well.) But educational leaders can't let a relentless inner drive to do everything flawlessly determine how they approach their careers. You'd be better served putting all of the energy you spend attempting to be perfect toward taking actions that will advance your career.

PERFECT DOESN'T EXIST

Like so many female leaders, I get caught in the comparison trap. I see flawless women—you know, the ones with a regular workout routine and great hair, or those who are involved mothers and well-respected leaders—and wonder how they do it all. No matter how hard I try, one of the balls I am working so hard to keep up in the air comes crashing down.

The truth, you might have guessed, is that despite appearances, no one is doing it all. Perfection does not exist (no matter what social media posts suggest!), and the pursuit of perfection is a fruitless venture. We will fail. We will fall. We will be too soft or too harsh or too emotional or too unsympathetic. The question is not whether we will struggle with our various roles and expectations. We *will* struggle. The question is, "How can we struggle in a way that shows self-love and brings us closer to those we love?"

Perfection does not exist.

The first step is to love your strengths—the good, the bad, and the ugly of them. That's right, strengths can be weaknesses, too. One of my strengths is that I am a peacekeeper and have deep empathy for others. Typically, that is a wonderful characteristic to have. But sometimes, as a leader, my desire for peace and my empathetic view can make me appear wishy-washy or inconsistent. What are your strengths? When do your strengths become weaknesses? How can you accept that these weaknesses are not flaws but simply obstacles to overcome?

I'm still proud of my empathy and tendency for peacekeeping, but I'm also aware of the ways they can hinder my leadership. So I've vowed to learn and grow every day, while accepting I will never "arrive." Not only is that okay, but it's also one of the great gifts in life: the opportunity to continuously evolve. When we start feeling inadequate or we find ourselves falling into the comparison trap, it is helpful to have a go-to mantra like, "I am enough." What mantra could you develop to remind yourself that you are wonderful just the way you are?

Perfectionists would do well to follow Laird Hamilton's advice: "Make sure your worst enemy is not living between your own two ears." Let's make our greatest champion the one living inside us.

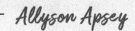
Allyson Apsey

STRATEGIES:

- Break out of the perfection trap.
- Love your strengths.
- Understand strengths can also be weaknesses.
- Know you are enough!

Practice Imperfection

We may know perfection isn't possible, but try telling that to our brains. It is a natural tendency to keep striving for perfect, but next time you catch yourself falling into this trap, remind yourself that it is a waste of both time and energy.

Think about all of the energy you could have spent on new projects or professional growth opportunities instead of perfecting a well-done project. There is a difference between "good enough" and "perfect" as a leader. Not everything has to be perfect—in fact, few things need to be. We encourage you to spend some time reflecting on what in your professional life falls into these categories. You will thank us later.

If your first reaction to the above challenge was to protest, "Everything must be perfect!" it may be easier for you to strive for 80 percent perfection. Most people won't notice the difference between your 80 and 100 percent perfection level. And remember not to point out the flaws you think exist because you didn't hit your 100 percent mark. We often think of weddings with this example. They always look incredible, but if you talk to the bride, she'll often note all of the small things that didn't go as planned. However, from the outside, those small details didn't impact the quality or experience of the wedding.

You might also find success by limiting how long you are going to work on a project. For example, how many of your friends keep saying they are going to write a book, but two years later find themselves no further along, fear driving them to endlessly tweak the proposal instead of turning it in. Identify a specific amount of time to dedicate to a task and then stick to it. Deadlines will help keep you focused and limit the amount of unnecessary hours you spend on something.

If you find yourself sliding into your perfectionist tendencies, ask for feedback from others. Often the work you think needs to be done truly doesn't. In that case, let it go.

BUILDING SELF-CONFIDENCE

Day in and day out, I doubted my decisions, my abilities and my leadership. Why did I feel that way? After all, I was appointed to this position because I had the vision they were looking for in the next leader of this school. I really did have what it takes to be successful. Looking back on this experience, I realize that, at the time, what I was really lacking was self-confidence. This is not something that you build overnight. Self-confidence comes with an investment in self. It comes with accepting challenges and finding solutions. It comes when you believe you can. You build yourself up on a daily basis and surround yourself with those who believe you can.

Twelve years later, I can honestly say I am still working on gaining the self-confidence I need in this position. I attribute this to the fact that, many times, I have not been given a seat at the table to share what I think, know, or feel. I have not always spoken up when I disagreed with what was being said or proposed. In other situations, I have spoken up and advocated for what I believed in, even when it was not well received. I have grown so much and gained more self-confidence, but only because I now refuse to sit idle.

I know that the best way to grow as a person and a leader is to take on new challenges. I have grown my professional learning network in so many ways because I figured out how to get involved in different ways to make a difference and advocate for what is right in education. I know I am not alone in this journey. I choose to persevere even when the outcome may not be what I expect or want.

 *Jennifer Black*

STRATEGIES:

- Ask for a seat at the table and take action for the good of the system.
- Be involved in your local, state, and national associations.
- Grow your professional learning network (social media, professional conferences, professional organizations).
- Positive self-talk daily (preferably in the mirror).
- Lead with integrity.

Realize You Don't Need to Be an Expert

Everyone likes to feel successful in their job, and educational leaders are no exception. We like to know we are doing well and making a difference. So we focus on mastering skills needed for our current position instead of gaining the knowledge and experiences we might need down the road. In their book *How Women Rise: Break the 12 Habits Holding You Back*, Sally Helgesen and Marshall Goldsmith say mastering every aspect of their current jobs can hold women back. In fact, in her book *Radical Candor*, Kim Scott shares how important it is for leaders not to block their rock stars from being promoted based on their strengths, and to remember that some rock stars don't want to be promoted but want other leadership opportunities within their current role. Don't get us wrong: We're not suggesting you slack off or phone it in. But we do encourage you to shift your focus to the jobs you'd like to hold in the future or find other avenues of leadership in your current positions.

Don't Fear Failure

The unofficial motto of Silicon Valley is "Fail early and often." Becoming familiar with failure—and the fear of it—is part of the success equation. We get knocked down, lift ourselves up again, learn, grow, and repeat. This process of recovering from setbacks is known as *resilience*, and it's key to succeeding in leadership.

Becoming familiar with failure—and the fear of it—is part of the success equation.

If we take failure out of the equation, our growth rates decrease dramatically. Doing so ultimately holds us back as leaders. While failing isn't the sexy part of success, it does help us learn what to avoid or tweak for next time. (Thinking of potential failure as a teaching and learning tool may help you move past fear.)

While you may think these moments only matter to you, your clash with failure has a much larger impact. When you embrace your struggles and view them as positive components of the success equation, you serve as an example to those who surround you and look up to you.

BE BRAVE

Having grown up in a traumatic household, I'm no stranger to challenges. My life might've turned out differently if I were the sort of person who gave up. But as I got older, I learned something about myself: Challenging situations don't define us. They can even make us stronger.

When I was a teenager, I made the conscious decision to leave the troubled life I knew. I set goals and developed plans to achieve them. I faced a lot of challenges and setbacks, but if my childhood had taught me anything, it was resilience.

In all my lofty goals, I gave myself permission to fail. Yet I refused to let myself give up. I pushed forward, my target always in sight.

As a teacher and a principal, I've shared this message with my students and staff to help them understand that it doesn't matter where you come from or what challenges you've faced. What matters is where you are going. I try to lead as an example of this: When I make a mistake, I don't give excuses; I own it and work to fix it. I want students and staff to know that all of us will struggle and fail over the course of our lives, but our failures become lessons that lead to our goals. If we are afraid to fail, we will never get where we need to go.

Had I quit at the first sign of struggle—a hard home life grow-ing up, competition with coaches for teaching positions, a scarcity of administrative jobs, and positions lost to male colleagues—I never would be where I am today. I was the first in my family to earn a col-lege degree. The first in my extended family to receive a doctorate. I have devoted twenty-nine years to the public education sector and received several awards for outstanding service in education.

Women leaders must replace perfection with bravery. Instead of seeking out situations you know you'll succeed in, take some risks and be brave with your actions.

Doreen Martinez

STRATEGIES:

- Pay no attention to your inner dialogue, which will try to keep you in your comfort zone. Listen to your gut instead. When you feel the butterflies and nerves kick in at the thought of trying something new or chasing your dreams, take the next step forward.
- Don't run yourself ragged trying to be brave in every situa-tion. Bravery takes lots of energy, so schedule time for daily self-care: workouts, meditation, and other practices that pri-oritize your health.
- Utilize a mindset that fosters the belief that you can change and grow.
- Just because you aren't there now, doesn't mean you won't get there eventually with work.
- Say yes! Instead of reacting to a challenging request with a "no," signifying your fear of failure, shift your thinking to a "yes" approach and work to make it happen.

Majalise's Story

GET BACK UP

The key to finding success is that you have to find failure time and time again. The more you fail, the more you learn. As we all know, getting back up after failure can be hard and takes strength.

Instead of viewing failure as something you must avoid or something that sets you back, we invite you to shift your thinking to view failure as a redirection of energy. During these moments, you just have to keep moving. While you might be tempted to throw in the towel, think back to your "why" and have the courage to keep fighting. Sometimes you might need some help to pull you back up, so don't hesitate to seek guidance or resources, or ask for help when you find yourself struggling or in the midst of a learning curve.

These principles don't just apply to big setbacks, like job loss. Life as a leader is filled with small daily setbacks as well. The spring of 2020 was a challenge in itself. The coronavirus pandemic, and the resulting shift to remote learning, demanded students, teachers, and families change how they view and interact with education. When my district decided to transform its in-person professional development into a two-hour virtual experience, I offered to make the introductory video.

It took an exploration of multiple platforms, frantic text messages to teachers, an argument with my educator husband, some explicit word choices, the slamming of my computer lid, and a full nine hours to make a fifteen-minute video—that almost didn't happen.

An hour into its creation, I contemplated saying, "Forget it." I could send everyone in the district a video conference link to watch me give the presentation live. I went downstairs, feeling relieved, and saw my husband working on a math lesson for his students. Then I gave myself a stern talking-to: "Do the hard things all of the teachers are doing and figure this out!"

I headed back upstairs to make that video. I am honestly not sure if I have ever been prouder of something I have made, but I didn't quit.

I shared my video with all of our secondary schools, and was even able to accept a compliment afterward.

Majalise's Story

THE UPSIDE OF SETBACKS

Leaders have to be real. We have to be raw. And we have to be in the moment—whether good, bad, or hard. When we are brave and take risks, we put ourselves out there in a new way that demonstrates our love for the profession, for others, and for our staff and students. Sometimes that is really easy; other times it rocks us to the core. We have to have patience and resilience to truly be able to experience the joy that comes when things start to come together.

Believe it or not, each moment leads to joy (yes, even the crummy ones). When explaining the idea of joy to my third grader, I had to make it tangible on his level. After his favorite doughnut shop closed, he was really sad. He patiently waited for the reopening, and when the date was announced, he was happy—even giddy, if you will. However, when the moment came for him to bite into his long-awaited dough-nut, he experienced pure joy. He hadn't settled for a boxed doughnut to replace what he was longing for. He wanted a fresh doughnut, and he waited. For a nine-year-old, it takes patience to avoid settling.

Leaders have to demonstrate that same patience through set-backs and challenges as they strive for their dreams. When a leader takes over a building, they have goals and ideas. In our experience as female principals, we instantly felt we had things to prove. We had goals for building achievement and were focused on reaching them quickly. This is not always possible, though, and setbacks do happen along the way. By staying the course and treating setbacks as oppor-tunities to continue to grow, the moments of success (for example, model-school status and increased graduation rates) brought joy to our entire schools when we had the patience and resiliency to lead with the organization, rather than taking setbacks or successes personally.

Silence Negative Self-Talk

Taking risks—and experiencing failures—takes mental fortitude. You have to be able to defy your doubts, take chances, tune out negative voices, and weather outside forces like school board politics or state-level changes. In order to be a true leader, you must be mentally tough. And to do that, you have to rein in your negative self-talk.

When you truly slow down and listen to your inner voice, you might find you are your harshest critic. Your self-talk may be unhealthy and unproductive, such as telling yourself you will never figure out the master schedule, that your staffing will never make instructional change possible, or that you are stupid for making a small mistake like forgetting to email an update to staff regarding a schedule change.

While changing your inner voice often takes years of work as you unpack habits and thought patterns, it is worth addressing and focusing on. Remember that things are happening for you, not to you. When you have a negative thought, such as about how a particular task is impossible for you to accomplish, you might try to reframe it into a positive. Shift your thinking to how this impossible task is going to push and grow you in a way you haven't yet developed. We have both found that journaling and reflecting on common themes we've identified within our self-talk to be extremely helpful. Over time, you will notice patterns, and having this awareness makes reprogramming your inner voice much easier. And finally, you might think about seeking out professional guidance or an accountability partner. When you do this work with the support of another, the growth rate increases dramatically and it helps keep you moving in the right direction.

Majalise's Story

DON'T DWELL ON YOUR MISTAKES

I think one of the most important parts of failure is recognizing it and moving on. Ruminate too long on a mistake, and it begins to affect those around you. That's what happened one day during an after-school tutoring session I was leading as a building principal. When I showed up late, a student and his dad were there and waiting, a strike against me in a string of events that had gone poorly. As I was throwing myself around the room, slamming drawers while looking for a pencil, the student said, "Ms. Tolan, are you alright?"

I didn't even try to pretend. "No," I said, explaining how I'd failed to stay calm during a terrible interaction with a parent. How I needed to call and apologize. I asked, "Have you ever just made a mistake, and as soon as you realize it, you want to take it all back?" His response was priceless and humbling. "Ms. Tolan," he said, "you have no idea."

When we make a mistake, we often overanalyze it to make sense of the situation. That leaves us exhausted, frazzled, and lacking confidence. When you're fixated on an error, specifically identify it, and work to let it go. Say "let it go" out loud to help you remember. The times you truly can't get an event out of your head, try talking it out with someone, journaling, or exercising. These approaches can truly make a difference in being able to move forward.

Majalise's Story

DON'T ASSUME YOU DID SOMETHING WRONG

I have a terrible habit of hearing blame when there is none. A supervisor will ask me how it is going, and I'll respond, "Why? What's wrong?" I didn't realize I relied on this response until a principal pointed it out. "I really just want to know how it is going," he said. "You always lead with 'Why?' If something is wrong, I would tell you."

After that interaction, I became increasingly aware of my tendency to assume I've done something wrong. Soon, I realized that fear—of not being perfect, of having made a mistake—interfered with my desire to share good things or engage in conversations that would help me grow.

My assumptions also resulted in a whole lot of apologies I didn't have to make. True, there are times you'll need to say you're sorry. Leaders make tons of decisions, and sometimes we get it wrong. When that happens, it is imperative that we authentically own our mistake and apologize.

That said, "I'm sorry" is probably one of the most overused and incorrectly used phrases. A leader should not apologize for following policy, providing constructive feedback, or making necessary, although unpopular, decisions. You may be sorry for your wording or delivery, but you do not need to apologize for holding someone accountable.

We believe it is critical for women to take risks to advance their programs, buildings, districts, and careers. Risk-taking can be just that—risky—but without taking risks, we run the chance of listening to the negative talk around us and our own self-doubt. Taking risks requires us to weigh the outcomes and prepare for some failures, but each risk moves us forward, and even if we fall, all we have to do is channel our strength, get back up, and take another step.

CHART YOUR PATH

⚓ When you find yourself in the perfection trap, what are some go-to moves you might try to embrace the failures and mistakes?

⚓ What is one area where you can take a risk to grow as a leader? What does that risk look like? Who can support you in that process?

Chapter 8

Make It Happen

Let's make it happen, ladies!!!! As we let go of our perfectionism qualities, it is time for us to roll up our sleeves and get to work. We are going to stare down inequalities in hiring and land the leadership role. We must stay motivated, lean on those around us, and trust our instincts if we want to succeed!

────────────── *Rachael's Story* ──────────────

HARNESS YOUR MOTIVATION

Growing up, I watched my sister with jealousy as she cranked out perfect test scores and took on challenges with ease. She was incredibly smart, had her act together, and made learning look effortless. I constantly cried out in frustration—I would never accomplish things in life, unlike my sister.

Luckily my mom used these moments to help me see that perfection wasn't a requirement for success, but motivation was. She always said I would go far in life if I stayed highly motivated and continuously worked to improve. While I thought my mom was placating me at the time, I am glad I trusted her guidance.

Over the years, I have come to realize her words of advice were spot on. Perfection can prevent you from taking steps toward success. Motivation and consistency, on the other hand, will help you move forward and get there.

Motivation isn't the same for everyone. Find what motivates you—increased student participation, highly engaging family events, a staff meeting led by teachers—and use that motivation to make decisions that will improve your culture.

Emotions aren't always predictable, and positive emotions can keep us moving when things are difficult. Know exactly where to go in your building or district to engage your positive emotions. Not everything we do will ignite that positive feeling, but we can take breaks to reengage with positive emotion.

On those days your motivation is lacking, take advantage of a "state changer." Take a walk, work from a new location in the building, and reflect on success to reengage the motivation that has led you to this point.

TACKLING YOUR TASKS

Women who lead, at any level, work more hours than their male counterparts. And I am not just talking about the hours at school. We might be shuttling kids to and from sports practices and events, planning dinners, or making plans for the weekend. We could be checking in on a parent, grandparent, or close family member. Maybe we are busy with volunteer commitments at our church or with community events. Whatever we do, we put in more than our share of time working for others, and that can leave us with no time for ourselves.

As someone who for years thought servant leadership meant serving until exhausted, I am learning that I need to prioritize myself.

When my anxiety is too high, my confidence at a rock bottom, or my emotions unstable, I can immediately pinpoint what is wrong: I am not taking any time for myself.

In order to lead well, you have to lead with intention. Take time regularly to map out your goals and plans for work and life. At least quarterly, I map out goals in four quadrants of life: professional, personal, passion, and position. I'm careful to set SMART goals—those that are specific, measurable, attainable, relevant, and time-based—and to do weekly check-ins on progress.

Utilizing a weekly schedule and creating an ideal week helps me prioritize tasks and keeps me focused on a clear timeframe to accomplish them. Most recently, I have found the importance of meditation or yoga in my regular routine. Learning how to breathe, reflect, and—gasp!—relax has also helped me recalibrate when my emotional regulation is out of sorts due to stress, difficult meetings, or unforeseen circumstances I have to navigate.

Doing too much equals getting nothing done well. Stop trying to be the woman who can do it all. (Spoiler alert: you can't.) Put away your phone, close your laptop, and participate in a meeting without distractions. Take handwritten notes and brainstorm plans and projects on large Post-it pads. By eliminating the noise, you can focus more deeply on the big ideas and be more present and aware in your surroundings.

Multitasking at home is just as unproductive. My boys can attest to that. If I am staring at my phone, I have no idea what they are talking about. I am terrible about doing something while watching a TV show or movie. Even while walking the dog, I can be found talking on my phone. Taking time to be fully present at home might mean you have to answer those emails later at night (or even tomorrow morning), but it gives you an opportunity to deepen your relationships with your loved ones and recalibrate your roles. Do you want to be remembered for sending that awesome email at 7:45 p.m., or for playing that extra game of Uno with your child? Speaking from experience, Uno wins every time.

Don't downplay all you do. You are juggling responsibilities at home, at work, and in life. You continue to set the bar higher for yourself and others around you. A dear friend stopped me once after he attempted to pay me a compliment. He said, "It is okay to just say thank you." Stop undercutting your value or the work you are putting into what you do. You work hard and should take a moment to accept the compliment, without excuses. The work you are doing can only be done by you, and when you do it authentically it is pretty amazing.

Jessica Cabeen

STRATEGIES:

- Plan, prioritize, and breathe. These are three things to repeat throughout your day, week, month, and school year. Make a plan, prioritize the work that needs to get done, and then don't stress about it. Remember to breathe, as it will all work out.
- Multitasking produces mediocre work. Instead of trying to do multiple things at the same time, such as answering emails while being on a Zoom call with your camera off, while answering a quick phone call, simplify your actions. Focus on one thing at a time.
- Don't diminish your greatness. You are doing great things. Instead of tearing yourself down, work to build yourself up for all the incredible things you do.

Majalise's Story

DON'T BE AFRAID TO DELEGATE

As we move into leadership positions, we take on more responsibility. With more tasks, projects, meetings, and oversight heaped on our plates, we need to take time to slow down and reflect on what has to be reassigned to others. Utilizing support staff is often an awkward adjustment for leaders. They often feel like they are delegating work they should personally be doing, especially if they know how and have the time.

Don't confuse taking something off your plate for a sign of failure. Instead view it as a sign of growth. After all, without this step, you will be spread too thin, stressed out, and incapable of doing a high-quality job.

I am terrible at asking for help. As a high school principal, I knew the administrative assistant in our front office was incredibly busy, so I dreaded asking for her help when I needed copies made, appointments scheduled, or support in completing other tasks. As a result, I'd end up asking for last-minute help while I scrambled around, which impacted her day.

One day she finally spoke up. It bothered her that I wouldn't ask for help, especially before I got so stressed. I felt terrible! Yet even after I explained my reluctance to add extra tasks to her already busy day, she wanted me to ask. Together we made a plan to meet regularly to plan for big events that would need her help. I am so thankful for her guidance and honesty. I am getting better at delegating tasks, and this learning moment impacted how I move forward with coordinating my daily work with others, delegating, and relying on support staff.

Learning how to manage our office staff of like-minded women wasn't easy for me. I had to have a conversation with support staff about roles and responsibilities. Passionate people do great work, and without my clarity, ours did work right over the top of each other. I also had to communicate more to discuss distribution and assignment of new or special-event tasks. Finally, by meeting weekly with support staff to check and connect, I was able to improve on my communication and decision-making to support our office in being more efficient and in better understanding and valuing the incredible work it took to run our office to support our staff, students, and families.

INNOVATE!

So often in education women are fearful of leading change that impacts the status quo and embarking on "outside the box" thinking. Whether a result of experiences of being denied opportunities or the subconscious desire to be accepted, we tend to cower from being perceived as an aggressor or change agent. I have found that when new ideas are followed through with actionable steps to get to the desired effect, others tend to find more value in them, which has built up my confidence over the years to disrupt education. Simply asking the right questions can lead us to innovate our practice for our kiddos. Now, "innovation" can be a loaded word in education. I don't mean bringing in technology or robotics, I'm referring to innovation regarding systems and processes. The most achievable way to get there is to be brave and bold in doing what is best for kids.

When I first came to Vero Beach Elementary as a brand-new principal, I was tasked with taking on a predicted F-rated school midyear. There were over a thousand referrals for student behavior and the school had nine substitutes rotating daily through classrooms that had been abandoned by qualified educators. The support staff and coaches carried radios to respond to calls for explosive behavior episodes and elopement. However, no one was really addressing why this was all taking place. It was reactionary at best, and the community had lost faith in the school. We needed change, and we needed it fast. It required us to look at our data and create a root cause analysis.

It didn't take long to acknowledge that the students were entering escalated in the morning and all being placed in the hallways of the school to feed off each other's angst. We started by asking "What if?" Could we live with moving the students into classes earlier and see if that helped calm our tier-one instruction? The teachers were brought in immediately and simply wanted someone to lead the needed change. We saw an immediate improvement as a result. Students were entering much calmer and having time in the classroom to read, play games, and socialize together before the academic expectations were set. The collective was greater than the individual, and in that case, it paid off for our entire school community.

Being brave and bold enough to challenge the ideas of what elementary was "supposed" to look like allowed for us to really reimagine other parts of the school. We established weeklong specials to help students build relationships with our special-area teachers, while creating more interest-based electives for our fifth graders to cultivate leadership and exploration skills. The result was a full fifth grade band program, sports program, science and robotics, and an art exploration elective. These simple changes resulted in deescalated behaviors and widespread change.

We continued asking "Why?" and "What if?" as a team. We modified our lunches, built in weekly principal book-group time, and established after-school office hours for our families, so that during the day I was able to improve instruction the best way possible, through feedback and observation cycles. We didn't ask permission; we just did what was needed to positively impact students and create an unwavering commitment to move the school. In just four years we were able to see a decline in behavior of 92 percent, and we moved the school ahead two letter grades. We openly chose to innovate systems to do what was best.

Cindy Emerson

STRATEGIES:

- Conduct root cause analyses of areas of need.
- Get buy-in from stakeholders by including them in the problem-solving.
- Create an action plan with clear steps for implementation.
- Create a culture of accountability to ensure steps take place.
- Celebrate growth and change frequently and publicly.

Have a Sounding Board

When preparing to make a huge decision, successful leaders rely on outside opinions, not just their own. If you're planning an important project, reach out to others to see what they think. You may look for confirmation you're making the right decision. You might poll everyone to find out their thoughts, then go with the majority. Or maybe you'll gather feedback and think critically about your options.

Seeking input is vital, so be a bold conversationalist. Critiques are healthy when they come from people we value and respect, even if we disagree with them. In *Dare to Lead*, Brené Brown discusses the need for what she calls a "Square Squad." These are the people whose opinions matter. These folks will be honest with you and love you regardless of your mistakes, imperfections, and vulnerability—but they won't suck up to you or tell you every decision you make or action you take is great. If you haven't identified your Square Squad yet, we invite you to do so, and to use them to practice delivering a decision. Finally, we encourage you to reflect and adjust; the folks who were on your Square Squad five years ago might be different than those who are on it now. We must constantly be reflecting and adjusting.

———————— *Rachael's Story* ————————

ACT NOW, ASK FOR PERMISSION LATER

When I left the middle school level and became an elementary principal, my superintendent gave me explicit directions: "Fix it." There was a lot of work to do, and my target became clear when I considered culture, student achievement and growth, and attendance. The first three years were a huge lift with staff, students, and families as they worked to turn the building around and address the myriad systems and structures that needed help. Instead of asking for permission for each change within the building, I knew what needed to be done and we did it. Yes, I kept my superintendent updated through monthly one-on-one meetings, but I typically addressed changes I had already made.

Leaders can get so bogged down with fear and asking for permission that progress slows and our ability to respond to students, staff, and the community is limited. For instance, a new leader might worry they will do something their boss dislikes, or they will get in trouble for not asking. We are not suggesting you skip the chain of command in your district as you roll out a new idea, especially if your supervisor prefers to be kept in the loop. Instead, we encourage you to stop looking around for people to give you permission to be your best self, personally and professionally. Approach your supervisor for feedback on your decisions as opposed to asking permission prior to moving forward. In fact, asking them when you begin working with them how they prefer to be kept in the loop is a great first step.

Stop looking around for people to give you permission to be your best self.

In the book *Get Out of Your Own Way*, Dave Hollis talks about the impact asking for permission can have on our life goals. "If someone does have a problem with something you're doing, it is likely they are challenged by it, feel insecure because of it, are jealous of your willingness to chase after it, or are frustrated that your belief in yourself makes them more aware of their disbelief in their own ability. In the end, it is rarely about you."

You may not need to ask for permission to take action on an idea, but you do need to plan well for each event, project, or idea you tackle. Glitches will happen. And when an event, project, or idea is new to a building or district, there is going to be speculation and doubt about how it will go. To finish a project at a high level, you will need backup plans for your backup plan. Skeptics will be on your side when things go right.

TRUST YOUR INSTINCTS

Eight years ago, I began my first principalship. I was not new to administration, but as a young female administrator, I had to quickly learn to be strong, confident, and courageous when confronted with doubt in order to fight for what was best for the kids. I can't tell you how often people treated me as inferior, maybe because of my age, maybe because I was female, maybe both.

I was my school's fourth principal in five years. The staff and community did not have a lot of trust in administration. I had to trust myself and lead with my gut.

At the time, the district office's curriculum and instruction director had been working closely with another school to create a literacy framework with a prestigious literacy guru. The director thought my school should follow the same framework.

My staff felt that they needed something different. They wanted to do something that was more efficient for teachers, a program that would yield quicker, better results with students. As a staff, we decided to get a research-based core reading program. In a twist of fate, my former district was retiring its core reading materials in order to purchase new ones. They gave us all of the old core reading program materials—at no cost to my new school or district.

Yes, my direct supervisor wasn't on board and was skeptical; however, I knew I had buy-in from my staff and that the program was research-based. With the backing of the rest of the district office, we decided to continue our work and focus on moving forward.

In about two years, with much training, review of data, adjustments, and additional tools, our school began outperforming all other schools in the district in reading at the primary grade levels. The district office couldn't help but notice. Our model of instruction was soon implemented across the district.

Don't let naysayers sway you in the wrong direction. If you know what is best for your students and staff (and you have backing from senior administration), stick with your mission and make your goals happen!

— *Tara Bourland*

STRATEGIES:

- Be confident in your decisions and back them up with research-based practices.
- Get familiar with John Hattie's work on effect size. Not every action has the same outcome when it comes to student growth.
- Trust your gut.
- Change is hard and people will doubt you along the way. If you get your staff to buy into the change process, great things will happen for students.

Own Your Achievements

As leaders, women can be uncomfortable using the word "I" and claiming success. We don't want to look like a jerk for taking all the credit, or we believe people should just know how much work we've done.

So we default to sharing the praise, crediting the team or entire organization. This makes us great team players and overall good people, but it does not help advance our career. When we skirt around our contributions, we discount all of the hours, thought, and work we dedicated.

Instead of dismissing and minimizing your work, or spreading the praise of your achievements around, look for ways to skillfully and gracefully promote your work. For starters, when someone compliments you on a job well done, say thank you—and don't say that it was something that anyone could have accomplished. Speak up for your contributions and qualifications. Own the fact you were named the principal of the year and share it with others. This is something to celebrate. If this makes you feel uncomfortable, enlist the help of a colleague to support you. When you have put work into making something happen, celebrate the success, including your important role in the process. Way to make it happen!

> *Speak up for your contributions and qualifications.*

CHART YOUR PATH

⚓ Where do you find strength in delegating and where do you still need to grow? What are some tasks you can commit to delegating? What will you now be able to accomplish because of delegating those tasks?

⚓ How do you handle owning your own achievements? If you do it well, how can you help other women develop that skill? If it is difficult for you, what are some ways that you can practice becoming comfortable with honoring your achievements and strengths?

Chapter 9

Magnitude of Decision-Making

Administrators make hundreds of decisions every day. Budgetary, disciplinary, professional, or personal, making daily decisions is what administrators do. These decisions come fast and furiously and range from what to have for dinner, what dress-up days to approve, or if the building needs to be put in a lockdown. Decision-making is one of the most important skills an administrator can possess, and it requires an ethical and compassionate mindset that allows for processing and reflection.

DECIDE TO LEAD IN THE NOW

What kind of leader do you desire to be? What kind of school do you desire to have? I've been a school leader for over ten years and this was not something I thought about too deeply until after a couple of years into my principalship. Yes, I knew I wanted to be a great principal who was supportive, knowledgeable, likeable, etc., and I wanted our school to be the best school ever. What I didn't know was how I was going to get there. I didn't stop to reflect on how my daily thoughts, actions, and decisions impacted my ability to achieve my desired goals. I hadn't learned how to take my attention away from what I didn't want, focusing on the things that weren't happening, and focus on what I wished to experience. How and what we think has immense power on the results we achieve. What we visualize and believe could make or break us as school leaders. "Leading in the now," what we do each and every day, either helps get us closer or further away from our desired outcomes.

Our mind is a powerful instrument. When we see and believe in what we want for ourselves, our students, our staff, and our school community, we learn to lead with clarity, focus, and intentionality. Visualizing what success looks like allows us to remove the emotion surrounding negativity, and instead, helps us to focus our attention on those leadership actions that will enable us to achieve our desired outcomes. Day in and day out, we must visualize that we already have what we desire. These daily visualizations are what will propel us to effectively lead in the now. Rather than hoping that we will achieve our desired outcome, or wishing that it will happen one day, we need to lead in a way as if it is happening to us now.

Leading in the now means that we lead and live as if we have already achieved our desired successes. We view ourselves with high expectations; having arrived at a place of proficiency as a leader. We are no longer trying, wanting, or wishing: we *are*. We are looking at ourselves through a lens of success where we already have the leadership capacity, knowledge, and ability. We go forth in confidence and an actualized faith that we can lead our team to success. So how do we do this? We educate ourselves and learn from others. We read, read, read. We attend conferences. We build our professional learning networks and learn from other great leaders. We listen to podcasts. We participate in Twitter chats. We collaborate with colleagues. The possibilities are endless, but the first steps are to visualize, believe, and lead in the now with purpose.

School leaders want nothing more than to work with a team that will go above and beyond to make our schools amazing places for our students and community. A place where students are loved, cared for, respected, and receive rigorous instruction. A place where innovation, collaboration, and trust amongst colleagues is the norm. A place where families feel welcomed, respected, and heard. The magic to making this happen comes from how we visualize our staff and school community. Leading in the now means that we see our staff as victorious, proficient, and exemplary professionals, and we treat them that way. When we do, they will not only acknowledge that you treated them this way, they will also feel validated as professionals. Professionals that will be willing to go above and beyond to support students' social-emotional and academic success. Students will no longer be wanting, wishing, and hoping to be scholars and good citizens; they will see themselves as already being scholars and overcomers of challenges and obstacles, such as poverty, abuse, neglect, or broken homes. With that feeling of victory, success and accomplishment, they can boldly go into the world as strong adults, advocating for change, strong individuals with high self-esteem, high regard, and respect for others.

As school leaders, what we choose to do today, how we lead in the now, either positively or negatively affects the results of our desired outcomes.

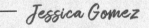
Jessica Gomez

STRATEGIES:

- Eliminate all negative possibilities. Focus on the positive.
- Visualize and imagine. Imagine and continue to imagine what achieving your goal looks like, feels like, what it is to be at the end.

- Encourage a risk-taking ability. Be comfortable with different ideas and suggestions. Give your team the trust, flexibility, and opportunity to change how we "do school."

Determine Your Decision-Making Frame

When making a decision, it is important for leaders to remember that their decisions will be viewed by others from various viewpoints. We have talked to women who felt their decisions were judged just because they were made by a woman, and sometimes that could be the case. But it is also a good idea to preview the impact of decisions to get ahead of possible judgment or unintended consequences.

Ethics: Administrators must always act with integrity and in an ethical manner. Resist the urge to gripe or gossip, whether in or outside of school. The ability to keep personal preference or biases in check is vital in all aspects of education, with administration being at the peak of fair and equitable decision-making. Acting in an ethical way should drive every decision an administrator makes and is never optional.

Position: Administrators wear many hats. It would be naive to think we check those hats at the door when making a decision, even if it is required when we put on our ethical lens. Our personal backgrounds and experiences provide a strength in decision-making that is important not only when thinking through the ramifications of a decision but also when planning the delivery of the decision.

As you weigh your options, consider the decision from a variety of viewpoints. Ask yourself: How would I accept this decision as a mother, sister, aunt, or daughter? How would I accept this decision as a coworker, mentor, or supervisor? How would I accept this decision as a student, sibling, or friend? By asking yourself these questions, you can anticipate how others will view your decision and craft your message with these answers in mind. It is not always possible to get everyone to agree with your decision, but it is always possible to work on the delivery of the decision to help others understand.

Loss: Every decision comes with a loss. That is not to say that all loss is the same, but it does exist. Majalise didn't really understand this until her mom, an amazing educator of forty years, broke it down for her. Imagine teachers have gone without being provided quality instructional materials for years. As administrators, we may assume that they would be overjoyed to learn we finally allocated the financial resources to provide high-quality instructional materials. And many would be. But consider an educator who has spent hours outside of the workday searching for and developing materials for her students, who has a lot of pride in her work and commitment. To have her materials replaced with a board budget vote and purchase order to the publisher may be painful. It is the leader's job to view decisions from the appropriate viewpoint to help navigate the change and support those most impacted.

As you make decisions, think about how they will affect those who might be losing something in the process. Consider: How might you help them with this adjustment? Are you prepared to provide time for staff, students, or families to adjust to the change and undergo any required training?

Place: Making a decision without considering the state of a place can be costly. Processing how the community, building, or media will react to a decision prior to delivering the decision is important. This is not to say that very hard decisions won't hurt anyone's feelings, but preprocessing ways to navigate the hurt and communicating transparently are essential. For instance, in a town that values music more than any other extracurricular program, reducing music offerings during times of budget cuts may be a decision to evaluate through the lens of place. Are there key communicators to discuss the changes with first?

Majalise's Story

PRACTICE SELF-CARE

Decisions are not always easy. It is wonderful when a decision we make is viewed positively. When the paper reports on the great news, we see it all over social media and we feel awesome. Sadly, we often make gut-wrenching decisions that anger or upset others.

The professional/policy brain and the personal brain aren't always on the same page. It's a real struggle—and not only for the decision-maker. My work decisions are confidential at home, but my family still feels the impact of a difficult decision. There have been times when I haven't come straight home, but instead hit the gym or the beach first, just to make sure I would be in a place to be a mom and wife when I got home. Other times, I have met another administrator after work so I could decompress before heading home. And there have been times I haven't done any of those things and have been a nightmare to be around. When that happens, I am thankful for my family's patience and grace as I navigate leadership.

Decision-making can be emotionally draining or invigoratingly rewarding and is at the heart of the leader's day. On days when decisions are especially difficult, it is important to remember self-care, find someone to talk to, go for a walk, or get a massage—whatever you need to do to mentally reset and unwind. After all, more decisions are waiting and will need your attention when you are ready.

Rachael's Story

CONSIDER YOUR PRIORITIES

COVID-19 stopped educators in their tracks. The typical approach to leading and running the school was no longer appropriate or safe. And since shut-downs happened with little to no notice, many leaders were left grappling for ways to address loose ends.

One such loose end in my building was finishing up a spring cookie dough fundraiser. Across Oregon, school administrators were given less than twenty-four hours' notice and little time to instruct families on how to handle collected fundraising money and forms. No sweat, we initially thought. We would have a two-week closure, then collect money and forms when we returned.

The temporary closure was extended to the rest of the academic year. Clearly we had some decisions to make regarding our loose ends: getting Chromebooks into the hands of our students for distance learning, handing back students' personal items, and making a plan for the cookie dough fundraising. These were tough decisions, with many families and leaders holding opposing viewpoints. While we worked through it, we made sure to identify the multiple lenses we were using to make decisions, and how these decisions would impact all stakeholders.

For us, we had to determine which lens of decision-making we were going to use. In this case, it was with our lens of place. Our decisions would directly impact public safety and health within our local community. We wanted to keep our students, families, staff, and communities safe and healthy. While we did end up canceling our fundraiser (and got the necessary items out to families), we explicitly communicated that the safety and health of our students, families, and staff were at the top of our priority list. The fundraiser was no longer important.

As you are faced with challenging decisions, stop and reflect. Why are you making this decision? What is the number one thing you want those involved to know? What lens of decision-making are you going to use? How might others view this situation and what pieces of information might they need to know?

MAGNITUDE OF DECISION-MAKING

I will always remember May 17, 2019.

It was my husband's law school graduation, the ceremony well underway. I'd stayed off my phone, listening to the speeches while distracting my three- and five-year-old boys with Lego blocks. I thought about how important the moment was—the amount of time my husband had poured into this degree and how proud of him I was. After the ceremony, as I waited for my husband, I received a quick call from one of my amazing assistant principals, who always keeps me in the loop when I am away. About five minutes later, my other assistant principal called. I remember being slightly irritated—it was a special day with my family, after all.

I answered anyway. He was out of breath. I could hear him sprinting as he said, "Molly, we have an active shooter in the FAB area. Kennon [a staff member] is out there." I ran through the list of protocols with him: Are we in lockdown? Have police been notified? Did you alert the district office? Is anyone hurt? He couldn't answer the last one.

Worrying about active school shooters keeps me up at night. Sometimes, as I walked the halls, I would run through how I would react if it happened at that moment. How could I keep my students and colleagues as safe as possible? I knew having a plan would improve my reaction.

The next call came five minutes later. Everyone was safe. But it was only the beginning of a traumatic incident we would be responding to for the next year. As students were in lockdown, my phone, email, and Twitter were exploding. One student who didn't know I was out of town emailed me asking me if I was safe. A senior who had my number called while hiding in an office, wondering what to do. My heart broke. I was awash with guilt for not being there that day, for being thousands of miles away and unable to do anything but reassure them. All I wanted was to hug them and tell them it was going to be okay.

There are no family pictures from my husband's graduation day. The rest of the trip was a blur of debriefing meetings via phone, text, email—communication with anyone who needed it. We flew out that night, and I went to the office early Sunday and watched the video footage, even though I knew it would be hard to digest.

Next, we met as a district team to decide on how to support students and staff when they returned to the building. We processed, focused on what our community needed moving forward and on how we would best support the wide array of needs we would see walking through the doors the next day. We had amazing partners come in who supported us and told us how to respond with our decision-making. I was so exhausted and overwhelmed with emotion that when I stopped at the store on my way home from that planning meeting, I left the car running the entire time, something I have never done before.

The following week was extremely emotional and challenging—and inspiring. My community did what my community does best: supported one another. We held a parent night, and I expected some hard questions. Our parents had gone through something no student or parent should ever have to be a part of. But all I received were hugs, handshakes, tears, and support. I expected at least one upset phone call or email. I would've understood that.

Many told me that you know you are an effective leader when things go smoothly in your absence. I did not find any comfort in this statement. I did find comfort in knowing my team evaluated circumstances and made decisions to support our entire school community.

Molly Ouche

STRATEGIES:

- When we practice, decision-making is engrained. Stay as calm as possible and run through the necessary questions to make the next decision.
- Communication is critical when making decisions. People may not always like what you do, but they will appreciate hearing about your process of why you did what you did.
- Inspiring moments can come in negative situations. Be sure to include those moments in your reflection process. We can improve based on our strengths as well as our weaknesses.

───────────────── *Majalise's Story* ─────────────────

GO WITH YOUR GUT

Forethought and planning are key elements of good decision-making—most of the time. Some situations, however, require swift thinking and decisive action.

When the call came in that there was a shooting threat at an elementary school in my district, I didn't have time to thoroughly weigh my decisions, no matter how critical they were. On top of that, two of the buildings' principals were out on family leave and the superintendent was unavailable.

As I got my high school into a code-red lockdown and headed to support the elementary school across campus, I kept in mind something a former superintendent told me: "If your gut tells you to do it, don't wait for the district office."

I realized upon seeing armed officers stationed at the door that there wasn't a single drill that had prepared me to weigh my options; those drills had prepared me to act. So I did. The other school leaders and I didn't make all of the right calls, but we made the right calls for the moment. We did what we needed to do to keep our students safe, support law enforcement, and work with families.

When the day finally ended, I realized I'd done the most important part of my job, the thing I always wondered if I could do. I'd faced a nightmare scenario—take care of other people's children or worry about my own—and decided with my gut to protect students.

I had trusted that those caring for my four children would put them first, and they did. In fact, my husband and three of my own children experienced the lockdown at their school that day and have their own terrifying memories. Our then sixth grader, in a dark gym full of students who'd planned to enjoy a science assembly, watched her teacher slowly approach the stage, where everyone in the gym could see boots under the curtain. The boots turned out to be those of a police officer working to secure an unlocked room, unaware the gym was full of silent students. The brave teacher was her dad. We all led with our gut that day and protected our children as if they were all our own. Because in the end, they really are.

Defeat Decision Fatigue

Decision-making fatigue happens to the best of us. You know the feeling: that of bone-deep exhaustion after making a million and one decisions all day long, and you just can't make one more. Perhaps it is approving a PTA fundraiser that competes with other schools' fundraising efforts and is sure to cause ripples through the community. Or maybe you have avoided getting back to your student council advisor because a simple yes or no answer is not going to suffice.

The problem with decision-making fatigue is that it can lead to decision paralysis. You have a choice to make, but fear or indecision has left you frozen in inaction. Whatever decision you are struggling with, know you have the solution within yourself. You can call a few friends to gather input and different perspectives, but at the end of the day, the decision lands with you. To help trust your gut in these challenging moments, meditate on the decision:

1. Shut your door and put your phone on silent.
2. Close your eyes and breathe deep.
3. As you reflect on the situation, go deep within yourself. What are your instincts telling you?

Whatever decision you are struggling with, know you have the solution within yourself.

As you determine the steps you need to take to move the decision forward, take comfort in the fact that your gut won't often lead you astray.

Rachael's Story

REFLECT AND MOVE ON

"That will be one hundred and fifty dollars, please."

My husband often jokes that I owe him money for my nightly therapy sessions, the moments I spend unloading the day's decisions and telling him how I am second-guessing all of them. Some days I come home so fixated on the decisions I've made that I can't let go of the day. I worry I've made the wrong choice, that it will make folks mad, or that I should have communicated the news differently. I can't stop breaking the decision down from every angle.

While you shouldn't fixate on or doubt your decision, it's a good idea to reflect on the impact it had and how others responded. Did you get a lot of parent complaints when you moved the fifth-grade graduation ceremony from night to day? Did your Facebook page blow up when you canceled a school fundraiser during the COVID-19 shutdown?

Take this feedback and reflect on how you might approach the situation again in the future. Would you make the same decision again? Was it in alignment with your past decisions and how you function as a leader? Before making this decision again, what else might you seek out to include in your decision-making process?

After reflecting, move on. Whatever your decision was, now is the time to own it. You did what you thought was best in the moment, given the information and perspectives you had.

Make Adjustments

We've already established we aren't perfect. It is a given we are going to mess up. We are going to make bad decisions. There will be things we didn't consider or impacts we couldn't have anticipated. Instead of kicking yourself over and over again, make another decision.

We were taught early in our leadership careers that there are times you have to make a swift decision, even if you're not sure it is the right one. Your inaction in the situation would be worse than a wrong decision. It is during these moments that we often dread we are going to mess up, which causes us to be paralyzed by fear. One way around this is to realize you can always make another decision to modify your initial one.

Perhaps you shouldn't have overstepped your student council advisor when you decided to cancel an event without checking with her first. But school was canceled due to a snow day and to hold an evening event on-site wasn't an option. You can still make things right by making adjustments to the event. For example, perhaps it can be rescheduled or modified to an online event so the community doesn't need to show up to the building.

As you deal with a bad decision, first take responsibility for it. Apologize to those affected, and don't make excuses for your actions. Ask others how your decision impacted them and hear them out. Then adjust the decision as needed to settle on a better solution. Take ownership for making the adjustment and why it was needed. This shows that you own up to your mistakes and rectify them.

Every day, leaders make hundreds—if not thousands—of decisions. Big or small, all serve to develop your trust within the organization. Sometimes we hit home runs, and other times we have new learning to do to improve our leadership practice. But every decision sends a message about who we are as leaders.

> *Every decision sends a message about who we are as leaders.*

CHART YOUR PATH

⚓ What are your priorities and nonnegotiable areas when making decisions? How do/can others know your priorities or what lenses you are using when making decisions?

⚓ When was a time you have reflected and moved on? What was a time where that has been a struggle. What were the differences in those situations that influenced your ability to move on?

Chapter 10

Knowing When to Move On

There comes a moment in every leader's career when they know it is time to move on. Maybe our views are no longer in alignment with those of the district or our bosses. Maybe our goals have shifted or our career plans have changed. It may be that we are being called to a new location and challenge.

Endings are a natural part of life, but we often find them the most difficult. That is, it's often hard to quit a job, so we put it off. In his book *Necessary Endings*, Henry McCloud notes that "today may be the enemy of your tomorrow." He goes on to explain that "the tomorrow you desire and envision may never come to pass if you do not end some of the things you are doing today." Don't let your fear of quitting a job cause your career to stagnate. There is an art to knowing when to move on, and there are three main times it's a good idea to call it quits.

Rachael's Story

WHEN YOU HATE YOUR JOB

"If you hate it so much, why do you stay?" This was the question I asked my friend over coffee during one of our statewide conferences. For the past thirty minutes, I had heard about all of the things that made her job difficult: the decisions she didn't agree with, the lack of appreciation, and how difficult the community was. She had brought up these issues time and time again, and it left me wondering why she stayed.

Maybe you have found yourself in the same place as my friend, working a job that infuriates and exhausts you in turns. Here's what I told her: You don't have to stay in a job you hate. Pause and reflect on your situation. Is it really that bad? Is it impacting your physical or emotional health? Is it causing your family and your close relationships to deteriorate? Do you hate the job or place you work? If so, don't try to stick it out. What's keeping you from looking elsewhere? During our chat, my friend pointed to reasons it would be difficult to move. She noted the insurance coverage we had, which was great, the paid parental leave, and the professional workday. However, the commute was killing her, she didn't feel supported, and her physical health was deteriorating. When she weighed out all that was in front of her, she realized it was time to start looking elsewhere.

While it might be scary to step away and apply for another job, don't allow fear of rejection or the unknown to hold you back. When you find yourself in these moments or patterns of negative thought, take a moment to reflect on your desire. What are your goals? Once you have identified these, know that anything is possible. Dream big and then map out plans to make a change. When you know what doesn't work for you, like

> Don't allow fear of rejection or the unknown to hold you back.

my friend was able to identify, it will help you better home in on locations that are a better fit for you and your needs. Finally, know that you always have options; you just need to keep your mind and eyes open, as opportunities are always around us.

─────────────── *Rachael's Story* ───────────────

WHEN THE JOB DOESN'T ALIGN WITH YOUR VISION

A new supervisor, whether joining your building, district office, or school board, can dramatically impact your work. Perhaps you were focused on proficiency-based learning but have to shift to a model that is not standards-based or focused on outcomes for kids. The job may now feel like an poor fit for you. Some of the best advice I received as I interviewed women superintendents for my dissertation was to make sure my mission and vision aligned with those of the people above me.

I have known many wildly successful women leaders whose new supervisors wanted to take things in a different direction. While they worked with those above them to come to a common understanding about the shift, many noted the job was no longer a good fit or something they could personally get behind. It is during these moments of change that we need to have enough self-awareness and bravery to move on. Sure, you could keep your head down and do your work as asked, but you wouldn't be living in alignment with your true self or calling.

As leadership changes, check to see if your mission and vision are still aligned with those above you. Do you share the same belief in students and in what school should look like? If not, it is worth having an open conversation with other leaders as you work to see clarity and guidance in the direction they are setting. If you find yourself out of alignment, reflect on whether the position is still a good fit. Just because a job seems ideal on day one doesn't mean it always will.

———————— *Majalise's Story* ————————

WHEN YOU'VE STOPPED GROWING

I became a teacher to work with students. I later realized what I really enjoyed was the responsibility of providing a positive experience for others. If I could impact 180 students every day in my classroom, I could only imagine my impact as a building administrator. I loved my district and my role, but I was eager for new challenges, and my ability to grow into a leadership position was slowed by internal hiring pathways. Hard as it was, I decided to move on.

At an interview for a leadership position at another district, someone asked where I saw myself in five years. I will never forget my response. It was probably the boldest answer I had ever given: "In five years, I will be the principal of the best school in the state of Oregon." I was applying for an assistant principal position, but my response made it pretty clear that my career plan was not to be an assistant principal forever. The interesting part of the story is that five years later I was the proud principal of that very school.

When you aren't growing anymore in your current position, it is time to move on. You need to be challenged, face obstacles, and encounter new problems. Does this mean you must leave your current position as a teacher, assistant principal, or district office administrator? No. But to improve the educational system for yourself and those you serve, you do have to find a way to be intellectually challenged.

———————— *Majalise's Story* ————————

WHEN YOUR DREAM JOB COMES CALLING

When I entered administration, my career moved quicker than I had planned. So when I was offered the building principal position at the high school—five years after being hired as an assistant principal at the same high school—I didn't know what to say. I wanted it, but I was very happy as an elementary/middle school principal, so I asked for some time to think about it. I had one hour.

I happened to be working with our church youth group, pulling vines out of a backyard. So I went back to work. I casually mentioned to my husband that I had been asked to take the position and had to call back in an hour. His reply: "Are you crazy? This is the job you have always wanted." He was right. I called the superintendent back to accept the job.

Even when we know who we are as leaders, we may be scared to push ourselves to our true potential or put ourselves out there. We are offered a job we have always dreamed of, but we are fearful of taking it. What we are doing is comfortable, and it's working for us. But it is time to start rocking. There is no easy way around it except to jump. Jump into the version of yourself you know exists. Jump into the job you are meant for.

APPLY ANYWAY

As a new assistant principal in my first admin role, I strived to live just outside my comfort zone, in the sweet spot where valuable and authentic learning and growth take place. With that in mind, I sought out opportunities that were just beyond my reach, stretched me beyond my expertise, and even scared me a little.

One such opportunity came in the middle of last spring. The principalship opened up at the school I hope to retire from. My husband attended the school as a kid, and I had spent the better part of a decade teaching and being a teacher on special assignment there. With less than a year of admin experience, I wasn't ready for the job—yet. After much contemplation, and despite understanding my complete lack of experience, I applied. It was my way of telling the district, "I want to lead this school . . . one day." It really was my dream job.

During the interview process, my fears were confirmed: I was in over my head! Needless to say, I didn't get the job. Regardless, I learned a lot through the process. And I had shown courage in stepping outside of my comfort zone.

In an unexpected turn of events, I was asked if I would like to become the assistant principal at my dream school. Naturally, I accepted. This opportunity allows me to learn from the newly hired principal, who has over 30 years of experience. And I've been paired with a mentor who is eager to support my growth and development.

Life and leadership are about continuing to pursue opportunities that challenge you and place you just north of your comfort zone. By putting yourself within your level of potential development and collaborating with more experienced and skilled colleagues, you can optimize your learning potential. Just think: had I let my fears take over, I wouldn't have applied or been given an opportunity to grow.

— *Sandi Battles*

STRATEGIES:

- Recognize the situation is happening for you, not to you. Opportunities to get to your dream job may not come around often and will require you to act quicker than you may have planned.
- Learn from the process. Apply for the job and experience the interview—you just might be surprised.
- If you aren't successful on your first try, don't let the dream die. Learn from it, put your learning to practice, and go after it again next time.

Rachael's Story

BE WILLING TO RELOCATE

When I first started thinking about becoming a principal, I discussed a job posting with my superintendent, who offered some sage advice about becoming an administrator. After suggesting I get a doctorate—which I initially laughed off, but eventually saw sense in—he asked, "Are you willing to move? How bad do you want this?"

At the time, I thought his question was kind of strange, but as I started to apply for jobs, I began to understand where he was coming from. Jobs will open up in your building and district, but that doesn't guarantee you will get them, so the wider the search, the more opportunities you will have. If you truly want to become an administrator and lead within education, you will find a way. You might have to move to another part of your state or cut your teeth in a building that will seriously challenge you, but you will find a way.

Leaders are needed across the nation, even in areas of your state that are less desirable for a variety of reasons. Women leaders are needed in these places even more. When leaving a job and applying for another, keep your eyes, ears, and heart open to communities you are called to serve.

> *Keep your eyes, ears, and heart open to communities you are called to serve.*

To get my chance, I had to move across the state of Oregon, into a community that was deeply challenged by drugs, generational poverty, and violence. However, my experiences there developed me as a leader and helped me find my passion for students who are underserved. If you find yourself stuck and blocked from moving to the next level, think globally. Where might you go to fulfill your educational purpose?

CHART YOUR PATH

⚓ What considerations do you need to make before moving on? Ultimately, how many of those considerations impact your leadership directly?

⚓ What is the most exciting thing about moving into a new leadership position? Who can help you find ways to employ that excitement as you move along your leadership path?

Chapter 11

Balancing Personal and Professional

M any women leaders find themselves tugged between work and their personal lives. They've been told it's an either/or decision: You can either be a rock-star mom or stellar leader. Gender stereotypes play a big role in women achieving home and work balance. In *Blindspot*, Mahzarin Banaji and Anthony Greenwald point out that the association of women with family and men with careers can be a subtle influence on a woman's decision to raise a family or seek careers.

We are here to tell you that you don't have to pick between work and family. Leadership isn't dependent on your gender. There are many incredible women leaders out there who are making time for their families as they are taking the leadership helm at the district, building, and department level.

Learning to adjust leadership to allow for home and work balance may be the most difficult thing to truly achieve because the needs of a growing organization or family unit are always changing. You probably won't achieve work-life balance all at once. The important thing is to reflect, communicate, love hard, and appreciate the moments you are in.

We are here to tell you that you don't have to pick between work and family.

REDEFINING YOUR ROLE

While the superintendency is filled with opportunities to make meaningful changes for students and staff, it is too far disconnected from both. Much of the day is filled with interpreting regulations, attending required meetings, negotiating contracts, and working with budgets and data. And planning—there are so many plans to be written! While all of these tasks are important, few make my heart sing or allow me to leave the office feeling fulfilled.

I became a superintendent as a thirty-year-old woman. I was high-energy, ambitious, and ready to take on challenges. All of these traits helped me in the work, but after two years I realized that I would need to redefine the role or risk burnout. It wasn't the hours or the difficulty—or even the severe budget cuts—that were draining me. It was that I didn't feel like I had a direct impact on the students and staff.

I'd gone into education to make a difference for kids, and I'd gone into leadership to ensure teachers had the necessary tools to provide strong experiences for students. Yet I could go weeks without seeing a student or a teacher if I didn't force myself into classrooms. Because I had entered the profession young, I was facing thirty years of this work. So I started looking for ways to directly connect with students and staff.

In 2011, four years into my work as superintendent, an amazing opportunity arose. I was fatigued from seeing our bright and talented students working minimum-wage jobs instead of graduating high school or moving on to college. Around this same time, science, technology, engineering, and math (STEM) careers were a hot topic, and I saw STEM as a way to help students redefine their futures. FIRST Robotics was the vehicle I chose to expose students to these fields.

I secured grants for a robotics team and put out a call for a coach. And heard crickets. I added to the lure with additional funding for technology, but still had no takers. My math/science-teacher husband took pity on me and agreed to coach the team under one condition: I had to be the assistant coach.

This one agreement likely saved my career in educational leadership. Prior to becoming a robotics coach, I was burning out, and quickly. Working with staff more directly had helped fuel me, and working to grow other leaders brought me joy, but neither of those things involved students. I was ready to leave the world of stressful meetings and furlough-day negotiations for the classroom.

By 2016, we had the highest percentage of FIRST Robotics students in the nation for a district with over a thousand students. Our program grew from the high school team to include full-continuum robotics programs for K–12. The high school team, FRC Team 4125, Confidential, has qualified for the world finals on numerous occasions, and each time, I've used vacation leave to be there with them. We take a yellow bus on all trips, even those across the country. I've driven the bus, I've ridden the bus—I've helped fix the bus—and through it all, I get to build relationships with students and listen to their advice and feedback on a variety of school issues. Robotics provides me with unparalleled professional growth and pure joy.

My work, and play, as a superintendent is much different from others. However, the collaborative work with staff, the time spent mentoring others and teaching classes, and the hours spent with students are what keeps me wanting to come back to the job each day. For me, self-care isn't a spa day. It's spending evenings and weekends in a shop full of kids working to build the best robot—and that's okay.

It's easy to read the job description of a role and fulfill the obligations. But to truly be a leader—and more important, a happy leader—we must redefine the role so that not only are we giving our best to the work, but it's also giving us something in return.

Heidi Sipe

STRATEGIES:

- When you are starting to feel burned out, pause to figure out why. What are you missing professionally? What is out of balance between personal and professional? Once you identify, intentionally work to spend time in your passion.
- Make the role your own. Don't let others define the role that you are filling.
- It is important to be a happy leader. Assess your happiness level and make sure that your schedule includes time to find your happiness.

Majalise's Story

FIND A WORKAROUND

An educational leader's job doesn't end with the school day. It can include after-school activities and evening commitments, which can be tough on leaders who are parents. When I was on duty at the high school, my husband and I paid our amazing daycare provider—who at this point is more of a family member—to watch our kids at the events. The support allowed my husband to coach and me to see our family while doing my job. I could take action when the bathroom at the stadium flooded or the fire alarm went off during the second quarter of the varsity basketball game. My kids had the joy of watching their mom work through hundreds of decisions just like those, and I was blessed to know they were being cared for while it happened.

Regardless of what is holding you back from being the leader you want to be, know that there is always a workaround. Worried about not having enough time with your own family? Bring them along to events and find ways for them to be involved, such as volunteering, cleaning, or passing out programs. Looking to balance nightly supervision of athletics, family nights, and activities with being active in your child's after-school activities? Perhaps you can help coach a sport or provide event management during your child's events, trading the other supervision times with others on your administrative team.

There are a few actions you can take when struggling with work-life balance: Work with the administrator team to support a night off when needed. Prioritize roles, jobs, and people to reflect your values and commitments. And find ways for your family to appropriately share in your joy at work.

WORKING MOTHERS

One of our more compelling human characteristics is our unique capacity to simultaneously serve in multiple roles. We can concurrently identify as sister, supervisor, and friend, each role bound by circumstance, yet none cancelling nor compromising the others.

But while people wholeheartedly embrace their own complex natures, they tend to see the world around them as dichotomous and singly purposed: other people are either one thing or another. This is perhaps most evident in how our social culture views motherhood and working.

One of the first questions I remember other adults asking me was "What do you want to be when you grow up?" While my answer changed throughout the years—veterinarian, scientist, doctor, teacher, lawyer, president, activist, event planner, and on and on—the one role I never explicitly stated, yet always implied, was mother. I never questioned nor imagined that I could not be both.

I grew up with a few nonnegotiable constants: faith, love, school, work.

Both of my parents were highly educated. Both were passionately dedicated to their careers. And both had somewhat specialized jobs that made it tough to find work in the same location. When I was very young, my father's research responsibilities often required that he live on-site for several months at a time. This meant we were physically apart during the week and together as a family every weekend.

Fast forward to when I was twelve. My mother received a promotion that required her to move across the state. It was an incredible opportunity for her and one that she had worked tirelessly for. My father, without blinking an eye, encouraged her to accept it.

This decision crystallized my views on what it means to be a working mom. My mother moved to an apartment in Houston, five hours away. She returned on the weekends and we talked on the phone every night. This rocked our little town. Women didn't leave their families.

Thirty years later, with two children of my own, I still get questions from well-meaning ladies who knew me back then: "How did you get over being second to your mother's job?"

I was not, nor have I ever felt, second to anything in the eyes and hearts of my parents. What I felt—what I witnessed, experienced, and learned—was unconditional love. My father loved my mother enough to not ask her to compromise her dreams. My mother loved my father enough to not ask him to compromise his. They loved my brother and me enough to model and serve as exemplars of humanity.

Through them, I learned that roles shouldn't confine your abilities; rather, your passions should help you define possibilities.

Even still, it would be dishonest for me to say that I haven't felt the pressures that come with being a working mother today. The disapproving glares, the hushed whispers, and the outright confrontations warning me that, at best, I'm missing out on my children's lives or, worse, I'm destroying their emotional, mental, spiritual, and educational well-being.

Real talk, friends: Not once in the seven years of my father working and living away from our family did anyone raise an eyebrow. He was applauded for supporting his family. Not once in those seven years did anyone ask my father who was taking care of his family or, worse, why he was resentful of his family. Not once in the eleven years that I have been a full-time mom has that been the experience for my husband.

Social stigmas can be debilitating.

My work isn't a job. It isn't a means to an end or even just a likeable hobby. My work is my heart's calling and I can still do it while being an incredible mother.

Brianna Hodges

STRATEGIES:

- Your role shouldn't confine your abilities.
- Let your passions help you define possibilities.
- Don't let others and their views of you impact your decisions when it comes to home and work.

Majalise's Story

LET THE PERSONAL AND PROFESSIONAL COLLIDE

When I was an elementary building principal, I would include a Principal's Corner message with helpful advice in my monthly newsletter. While I was encouraging parents to be actively involved in their child's academic life at home, I was super tired by the time I got there myself. Advising them to find spot at the table to do school work? We couldn't see the top of our table beneath piles of mail, books, and other junk. I knew I needed to read to my kids or have them read to me, but I was tired.

So I wrote a Principal's Corner that laid it all out: I am tired, and I don't want to read with my kids or check their work, but I don't have that option. I can trade with my husband, but he is tired, too. Someday my kids will be voting on the president of the United States of America and they needed to be educated. I put myself totally out there and waited. The result was amazing.

It turns out other parents were also exhausted. We all had permission to be tired and honest, but we had to suck it up and read with our children anyway. And guess what, it became easier. I stopped feeling guilty that I had one book memorized and would close my eyes, hold my son, and pretend to read it while he turned the pages.

Being a superstar at both home and work is hard. Many of us go home and are faced with a second shift of cooking, cleaning, homework with kids, and taking care of children or other family members. If you don't have these obligations, you might be faced with continuing education classes, walking the dog, or worrying about your personal life. We often try to leave all of our personal issues at the door when we come to work each day. The same is true for leaving professional issues outside of our personal relationships or home. In *Permission to Feel* by Mark Brackett, finding ways to regulate your emotions is an important part of being able to separate the professional and personal issues. I am blessed with a drive home along the Pacific Ocean. Although the effort is still a work in progress, I try to use that drive as a buffer between the things that pull me emotionally at work and the things that pull me emotionally at home. I use the ocean as a reset between the two worlds that I so often find trying to intersect.

How can you allow stakeholders and families to see or read about your authentic self as you connect with their students? Perhaps it is through social media updates, a newsletter, short videos that highlight behavior expectations, reading a story, or celebrating an assembly.

Part of being authentic is allowing your personal and work lives to slightly blur so you can function as a person with a life full of challenges, struggles, and triumphs—just like everybody else.

> *Part of being authentic is allowing your personal and work lives to slightly blur.*

Majalise's Story

USE PARENTING MOMENTS TO CONNECT WITH STUDENTS

When I was an assistant principal, my youngest two children attended a preschool and a daycare on my high school campus. As a principal-mom, this was a blessing and a curse.

On one occasion, I made a pit stop at the daycare side of the campus, which also housed my child's preschool, while taking a high school student to lunch. He had just finished letting me know that everyone in the school hated me. When we reached the preschool, two sweet (and very dirty) little kids ran toward me yelling, "Mom!" I hugged them both, turned to my student with a smile and said, "Nope, not everyone in this school hates me." The high school student smiled back. As we headed back to the office, I knew we'd connected. From then on, we didn't always agree, but we had a connection that showed we were both loved and worthy of compassion and grace.

Whether your children are in the same building with you or not, use shared experiences to make connections. Tell a funny story about your weekend or make a situation a little lighter by sharing similar struggles. Talking about your family and revealing your personal side makes you more human and authentic to those you lead—staff, students, and families.

Majalise's Story

ACKNOWLEDGE HOW YOUR WORK IMPACTS YOUR FAMILY

"Mom, is it the principal's job to go after the bad guy in a code red?"

"Ali, the principal helps keep kids safe."

"Mom, I don't want you to be a principal anymore."

This is the first and last real conversation I had with my kids about my job as a principal in a code red lockdown. It took place during one of my early years as a principal. From my kids' perspective, attending family nights and high school games was great. But the code red lockdown drill where the principal is responsible? This is where rubber meets the road in the mind of a second grader. Knowing your mom is responsible is not fun.

These conversations are hard and often have an added layer of mom guilt. However, naming the feeling, acknowledging it is there, and working through it with our loved ones can make all the difference in the world. If you find yourself struggling to acknowledge the effects your work has on your family, talk it out and share your feelings. Ask them how your position impacts them and share with them how it makes you feel. An educational leader's position affects the whole family, and each member will respond differently. It is important to talk about all of the implications of the position and to work together to understand the family's role in supporting each other.

Rachael's Story

YOU DO YOU

"If you had kids, it would make you a better educator." These were some of the harshest and most hurtful words a staff member ever said to me. True, I don't have kids. I have stepkids, who are older and out of the house, but I didn't birth and raise them like this teacher was talking about. That didn't prevent the words from cutting deep into my heart. My eyes welled up with tears. I told the staff member I needed a few moments and walked out of my office.

This teacher didn't know my first marriage wasn't a healthy one— that it was a good thing I didn't bring a child into the situation. She didn't realize that when I remarried, I was blessed with two stepsons, or that by the time I was ready to have children of my own, it wasn't in the cards, medically speaking.

Am I thankful for what I have? You bet. However, that doesn't make Mother's Day any easier or my responses to comments like this teacher's any less pained. My one wish is that folks would see and understand you don't have to be a mom to be an incredible leader and educator. You are perfect just as you are.

So for those bonus moms, stepmoms, hopeful moms, or never-moms, know that you are a fantastic educator and are maybe the only motherly influence some children ever know. My administrative assistant and friend once said, "You hold those babies tight when they are sad, you take care of them when they are hurt, and hold them accountable when it's needed. Hold your head up high and know that you are right where you are supposed to be and that you are the mom to many."

TAKING CARE OF YOURSELF

My health wasn't always a priority. For much of my career, I put others and my work before myself. And when I did take "me" time? I was often met with guilt, from myself and others.

I now make myself a priority. I take care of myself and my health, eat well, and get enough rest. At least three to five days a week, I spend an hour working out or doing things I love to help me de-stress. I practice yoga, run, spin, garden, and walk in the woods. If I only get in three days one week, I don't beat myself up. Life and work happen. There is always next week to try to make it up.

Balancing the professional and personal is hard. Because of this, it takes a lot of energy and focus, often leaving us feeling depleted and exhausted in our work. As women, we have to slow down and take time for ourselves if we are going to last in leadership positions. This means putting self-care high on our priority list and ensuring we are spending time with our family. Hard as it may be to believe, balancing the personal and the professional is possible.

Tara Bourland

STRATEGIES:

- Schedule in time to exercise each day or a few times a week.
- Be intentional when building your daily schedule. Create open space between meetings or throughout your day so you can reset and take care of yourself as the day progresses.
- Take inventory of what you are eating and drinking through-out the day. You might be in need of a reboot if you are only drinking caffeine and processed food.

While balancing the personal and professional is hard for women with families and kids, it is also tough for those without children or a spouse. Just because you don't have kids doesn't mean work-life balance is a breeze. Perhaps you are dating someone or have a side hobby that you keep pushing off to the side. As educators, we are drawn to serving others, and this often leads us to feeling burned out and empty. In order to continue to serve and be our best selves, we have to start prioritizing ourselves within our day.

CHART YOUR PATH

⚓ In what ways can you allow your personal and professional lives to blend? In what ways is that not possible?

⚓ Reflect on how you feel after a vacation or long weekend break. How can you recreate those moments in shorter increments to avoid burnout?

Chapter 12

Be Authentic with Your Leadership Style

One of the most common ways women try to survive in male-dominated positions is by working to fit in as much as possible. This means they attempt to act, speak, and lead just like men in order to become "one of the guys." Whether it is in Silicon Valley, on Wall Street, or in the district office, phrases like "old boys' club" and "boy in a skirt" are not lost on women breaking ranks in leadership positions. Where the waves are churning in education is in the realm of women leading through authentic styles of their own.

Rachael's Story

TO REPLICATE OR NOT TO REPLICATE, THAT IS THE QUESTION

It wasn't until I entered my first principalship that I realized how tricky it can be for a female leader to fit into a role created for and historically filled by men. Should we as women show the exact same emotion our male bosses modeled to us as teachers? Should we communicate the same way with our staff? Should we handle conflict the same way they did? These are all things I still wonder about today, and I'm not alone.

Many female principals and leaders struggle with the same challenge. When new to a leadership position, they try to recreate and replicate what they think people want from them without being authentic to themselves or their style. They model and emulate the leaders that mentored, trained, or supported them. This could be from a male or female perspective.

Because I didn't have a lot of female principal role models outside of my mom, I thought I was supposed to wear dresses and heels to work each day—things so far from my comfort zone they didn't even exist in my closet. After signing my contract, I bought all new clothes, but I knew I was trying to be someone I was not. While I like wearing skirts and dresses on occasion, I am all about the dress pants and the outfits that will allow me to sit on the carpet when helping with reading groups, go down the slide at recess, or rescue a kid who escaped the building.

Be true to yourself as a leader.

This evolution of understanding—the need to be true to yourself as a leader—can take a lot of years to reach. It can take a lot of wrestling and reflecting to honor the expectations supervisors and others have, while also finding a way to fit in and have an individual style. The reality is that leaders come in all shapes and sizes, with a wide variety of skills and abilities.

LEADERSHIP, YOUR WAY

Given the well-researched organizational success derived from such characteristics as empathy, selflessness, vulnerability, and attentiveness, why is it that women sometimes feel compelled to act like men in order to be taken seriously as leaders? Over the course of my journey in education, I've watched as many female administrators under whom I've worked have adopted traits that are stereotypically—albeit unfairly—characterized as male. They're emotionally unmoved and assertive to the point of being aggressive; they adhere to hierarchical power structures and subscribe to motivation through intimidation.

To be fair, many of the male leaders with whom I've worked have been extremely gentle, caring, and calm. Yet the stereotype still exists. And even more importantly, female leaders often still play into it.

In 2019, I was hired on as McMinnville High School's first female principal in 109 years. I was proud and believed it was something that was important to shine a light on, but I was also surprised by how big of a deal it was in our community. When I got the job, I was serving as assistant principal of the same school. Following the announcement of my hire, male and female students alike would fist bump me with comments like "It's about time!" The local and school newspapers ran stories with my gender front and center. To top it off, I was a 6A high school principal, the largest high school classification in Oregon, who was both female and under forty. That's apparently a pretty rare thing in the state of Oregon.

There were two prevailing sentiments that bubbled up in tandem: "This is something to be celebrated!" and "I wonder if this will work."

While on the surface, the welcome was incredibly warm from staff, students, and community stakeholders alike, some interesting questions emerged throughout the hiring and training process—ironically many from female superiors. These questions included whether or not I'd support athletics (interesting, as I was a college athlete myself), whether or not I'd be able to manage the budget (as someone with a doctorate degree, it would be pretty embarrassing if I couldn't), and whether or not I'd be able to balance home and work life (all of the previous male principals had to, too, but apparently they were not asked).

Being hyper aware of the microscope I was under, for the first half of my tenure as principal, I channeled a stereotypical male management style in an attempt to defuse the questions. I overly focused on facilities, carrying tables down the hall to the next event so I could be seen. I made the budget process extremely transparent so that every dime spent could be accounted for by curious parties—not a bad thing, but I was more focused on showing my money management skills than in putting the money to good use. Finally, I did a superb job of neglecting my family.

Here's the problem: I didn't get hired for any of these reasons. I got hired to be an instructional leader. I got hired because of my ability to compassionately serve both students and staff. I got hired to inspire big change. In an effort to prove myself and overcompensate for my age and gender, I was becoming a jack of all trades and a master of none.

Female leaders—all leaders—need to embrace their inherent leadership styles, even if they come across as softer, gentler, or more unassuming. Just as soft skills are some of the hardest and most important to learn, softer leadership is often the hardest but most important type to sustain. It is the kind of leadership that is founded in empowerment rather than control, and in serving rather than being served.

Amy Fast

STRATEGIES:

- Your job is not to follow the male leader you are replacing; your job is to be the leader you were hired to be.
- If you are the first female leader in your role, honor and celebrate that milestone, but don't bear the weight of all women on your shoulders.

- Be clear about your skills and use them transparently and unapologetically.
- Write your own narrative. Societal norms don't need to dictate it for you.

Visualize Your Authentic Self

Leading authentically is often one of the biggest challenges women face. We often feel pressured to fit in and emulate others as we work to thrive in professional environments. But you don't have to change who you are. You don't have to conform to the norm to be accepted. In fact, the skills and talents you bring to the table make you unique to the position you are in. If you are struggling to find yourself when it comes to leading as a woman, we recommend you spend some time finding out who you are and what you stand for.

You don't have to conform to the norm to be accepted.

Close your eyes. Imagine you didn't have any pressure or external expectations from others. How would you lead? What would it feel like? What would your interactions with others look like? As you feel your way through this exercise, consider what it means to bring your best self to your position. What part of yourself needs to be honored and not hidden from others in order to be the true you? Is it your sense of humor? Your love for having fun and building relationships with students?

Once you've identified and pictured your authentic self, connect it back to what you're currently doing. What is missing? What needs to be added? While it is easy to get stuck on why you can't lead authentically, we want to push your thinking to the things you can control. You might not be able to change a building's dress code or the administrator in charge of classroom observations, but there are ways to infuse your flair and personality into all you do. What might that look like?

Being authentic is easier said than done. You'll need take a risk, put yourself out there, and have confidence in what you do and say. Authenticity requires trust, and when you can't trust those around you, you have to fall back on the most important person to trust of all: yourself.

LEADING AS MY TRUE SELF

Connect. Support. Encourage. These three words are my passion—and the driving force behind my authentic leadership style. They best describe what I strive to do each and every day I am given the privilege and opportunity to lead. I work on embedding these into my daily practice and interactions with my staff, students, families, and colleagues.

In my daily work I am constantly connecting with staff, students, and families. I am a principal on the move—sitting has never been my thing, and the office is too removed from the reason I chose this profession: the kids. Conversations and personal interactions are my favorite part of each day.

It is my job to support others. I support students who may have experienced trauma or are struggling with friendships. I support staff members who want to grow professionally and often provide personal support as they experience the ups and downs of life. I support families on the first day of kindergarten, the last day of fourth grade, and everything in between.

Early in my career I was hesitant to seek support. Would it make me seem less competent? Would others think I couldn't handle the job? Fortunately, I have wised up and now know that support doesn't equal weakness. So often the support we find coincides with the connections we make. Case in point: the colleagues I've met throughout my state and across the country through state and national principal organizations. Support makes us stronger in all aspects of life. Don't avoid it—embrace it!

Encouragement might come in the form of a note to a staff member, a phone call to a family, a pep talk with a student. I find joy in encouraging others and seeing them grow. The encouragement I give may make the difference between a student or staff member settling for something or accepting a challenge.

Every August, I sneak into classrooms the night before the first day of school and leave each staff member a note of encouragement on his or her desk. It is my hope that this encouragement will serve as an inspiration. I love it when I am in classrooms and see those notes hanging up for the teacher to reread throughout the year. Those words, acts, and notes of encouragement are important for all of us. I, too, post notes from staff, parents, and kids in my office. I have a "memory jar" filled with notes from students; this is my go-to when I need encouragement.

As a female leader, I have learned over the years to connect with others, to give and seek support, and to encourage others with small but powerful acts. I have learned to embrace these to help me grow. Throughout my career, I have never lost sight of my passion or the three words that form the basis of my authentic leadership style: connect, support, and encourage. Time has only enhanced my ability to intentionally weave them into all aspects of my life, and I am better as a result.

Erin Simpson

STRATEGIES:

- Know that support makes us stronger. Ask for help and embrace it.
- Connections are key. Find your people to seek guidance and offer encouragement.

- Find your inspiration and passion in your building or district, and seek out opportunities to engage them. Make time to involve yourself in your passion.

————————— *Majalise's Story* —————————

LEAD YOUR WAY

As a leader, I have always been as real as possible with everyone. My life on social media is an open book—the good, the bad, and the celebratory. I am first and foremost a mom and wife, and I don't always excel at those two roles. When our family is a circus, I let people know. When I make poor decisions, I own them.

At times, this approach has demonstrated an understanding that navigating a family and work isn't always easy. People have known the high school principal's kids didn't get home for dinner until after 8:00 p.m., or she was late to a presentation because she got a flat and doesn't know how to change a tire. I have made a point to not hide my personal life from public view because I ultimately believe we are all in this together. I might be a decision-maker in the district, but I am only one person—a multifaceted woman who likes to eat grilled cheese, watch sunsets, and learn and grow. I don't shy away from conflict or questions, even when they hurt my pride or my heart. Without them, we can't ever really improve.

My transparent leadership style has left me pretty raw at times, and it's been painful. I've had to talk to my kids about how people may say mean things about me, but it isn't their responsibility to defend me, nor are those things a reflection on them. My husband has had to be a rock during hard times. Yet despite the difficulties, my position is rewarding, too: I get to make a difference in the lives of the youth within our community, including my own children's.

While being transparent and merging both my professional and personal lives works for me, it might not for you. As a leader, you need to figure out what leadership style truly fits you. Here are some steps that can help you figure that out if you haven't already.

- Identify your educational passions, such as early literacy, student voice, or thematic teaching. What aspects of education ignite a fire within you? How can you incorporate those things into your leadership role?
- Lead with your personality. Be you.
- Have someone you respect explain how they view your leadership style. Does their perception match what you are trying to reflect as a leader? If not, make a plan to incorporate their feedback into your professional growth.

Aim for Respect

In her book *Leading with Grace*, Jessica Cabeen has it right when she asks, "Do you want to be liked? Or do you want to lead?"

As women, we often worry about whether people like us. While likeability is a key factor in whether we get fired, hired, promoted, or demoted, it should not be all-consuming. Instead, we invite you to strive for being respected, as well. If we focus solely on being liked, we are completely missing the boat when it comes to respect. Interestingly enough, those who are both respected and liked achieve the most success.

There are ways to get over your deep desire to be liked. Realize your leadership style won't work for everyone. That's okay. Instead, dive deep into reflection to figure out where the desire to be liked comes from. Are you afraid something is going to happen if you're not well-liked, or did it come from childhood? Figuring out where it comes from can help you address the desire head-on. You might also try to balance your drive to have others like you by liking yourself. When asked to do something, don't just say yes out of obligation and a desire to be liked. Do what is right for you and your leadership ethics.

Finally, don't let other people's frustrations with you influence your leadership and decision making.

As you think about what your leadership style looks like, we encourage you to reflect on how it aligns with your personality and passion. Are there areas you could tweak to become a more authentic leader, such as demonstrating joy when students at your school accomplish goals? Are there areas holding you back that you could further develop, like how you communicate with others?

Our leadership style is truly a work in progress, changing and growing as we do. We can work with others to reflect on our leadership practice and compare their perception of our style against our own. It can feel harsh when you learn the leader you strive to be is not the leader others see, but this will allow you to take ownership and grow, strengthening your work as a leader and your ability to impact and influence others.

RULES TO LEAD BY

One of the first memories I have of wanting to be a leader is from 1989. I was watching an early screening of the movie *Lean on Me*, and I was completely in awe of the way Morgan Freeman portrayed Principal Joe Clark. It seemed that the real-life principal Freeman portrayed was drawn to challenging the system to show others that strong leadership could transform any environment. Taking over a failing school that had been forgotten by the system called for a tenacious leader and tremendous courage in the face of adversity. What others believed to be impossible, Clark willed to make possible.

Looking back on the movie, which I watch annually before embarking on a new school year, I am able to identify some of Joe Clark's leadership flaws. Still, I will always draw strength from the authenticity, courage, and vulnerability he demonstrated. These characteristics have made me the leader that I am today.

I would like to tell you that when I started my career these leadership principles came naturally, but that would be untrue. Throughout my journey, each leadership principle has been iterative, molded, practiced, strengthened, and refined. Moreover, the intersectionality of being female and African American has made my leadership journey an interesting one to say the least.

Navigating in both worlds means that I am sometimes fighting two battles as a result of my identity. My foundational core must be strong; knowing who I am and what I stand for is absolutely critical. Throughout my career, I've followed three main rules that have helped me stay true to myself.

RULE NO. 1: BE AUTHENTIC

Society has an ideal view of what women should be and how they should respond. Ideals are about a standard of perfection. I don't know about you, but I am not seeking perfection. I am seeking growth and truth in who I am, what I believe, and how I lead. Authenticity is our strength. The best thing you can do to break expectations is be your authentic self.

People like to know how leaders feel and where they stand with them. Be true to your core values and beliefs, and when challenged, be honest with yourself if you are wrong. We cannot be all things to all people, but we must be all that we are to ourselves.

RULE NO. 2: BE COURAGEOUS

During my career as school leader, I have sometimes found myself in a lonely place. Despite having great support people working around me, the buck does stop with me. When you're a leader, the negative voices, though few, can sometimes be so loud that they begin to drown out the positive ones. And then there's imposter syndrome, feeling inadequate and undeserving of our successes and accomplishments. All of this can cause us to question decisions we have made or prevent us from tackling hard issues with confidence.

In order to demonstrate courageous leadership, we must lead from our core values. When we know who we are, what we believe, and why we were called to lead, we can stand boldly in our leadership. Being courageous does not mean being all-knowing or above reproach. Courageous leadership is asking questions that lead to improved systems and structures, leading and engaging in challenging conversations, and, in times of great uncertainty, making decisions that may not be accepted by all.

RULE # 3: BE VULNERABLE

If you are being courageous, you must expect to fail. Failing is evidence that you are trying. If you don't fail, then you must ask yourself if you are pushing the envelope enough. Remember, seeking perfection is the enemy of being vulnerable. Experiencing failure gives you the opportunity to strengthen your leadership core. Through failure, leaders develop resiliency skills by learning how to pivot in a new direction. If we are not able to share our successes and failures with others, and unpack how those experiences have shaped us as leaders, we will not be able to be lead authentically and courageously.

The strength in the rules mentioned above means that your leadership compass will always be pointing in the right direction. By doing the necessary leadership work to ensure that your reasons for leading align with your daily actions, you are living your purpose. Leadership is not easy. Take the time to craft your skills, but more important, always remember to be authentic, courageous, and vulnerable. Lead well!

Sanée Bell

STRATEGIES:

- Be authentic: The best way for women to break societal expectations is to be themselves and lead with core values and beliefs at the center.

- Be courageous: Ask questions, lead difficult conversations, and have confidence when making the hard decisions.
- Be vulnerable: Share successes and failures with other women so that all can learn and grow.

One thing we can guarantee in life is that you are unique. There is no one out there exactly like you. Each one of us leads, communicates, and operates in our own unique ways with our special way of thinking. While it might be tempting to conform to the group, we encourage and invite you to find your authentic self when it comes to who you are as an educational leader. Aim for respect, be true to yourself, and know that you can't go wrong when you listen to your heart.

CHART YOUR PATH

⚓ What is your authentic leadership style? How do you describe it? If others described your leadership style, would it match your reflection?

⚓ How can you use your passion and leadership skills to influence other women leaders to follow their own passions? How can you use them to help you continue to follow your own path?

Conclusion

L
eadership is always evolving and our work is never done. The constant change, rapid decision-making, immersion in passions, and work to improve are exciting and leave leaders hungry for the next challenge and celebration to come. For women, the leadership journey is often a rocky and emotional one. It can be likened to a roller coaster ride, with ups and downs and twists and turns, and is best enjoyed with others around us. The shared experiences and connections with others are a driving force in improving ourselves and our schools.

Leadership can feel lonely, but should never be done alone. Finding a support system to help answer questions, celebrate successes, offer encouragement, and find professional growth opportunities and pathways is critical. There is nothing more exciting than sharing a success with others. As leaders, how often do we find ourselves not wanting others to know our successes, being humble to the point of neglecting to celebrate. We take great joy in celebrating others but need to stop long enough to celebrate our own ride, find inspiration in our own work, and find confidence in our ability to lead others, take that next step, and inspire more women down a path of leadership.

The process of writing this book required a lot of self-reflection and personal growth. It challenged our thinking, stretched our understanding of our own values and beliefs as women leaders, and made us both pause and reexamine how we were leading our own work in education. Were we really following our passions in the workplace? Through our research, reading the vignettes, and editing, we realized our own next steps on our leadership journey. At times, it felt overwhelming, but we weren't alone. Our network challenged us, inspired us, and encouraged us to become better leaders.

References and Books We Love

Achor, Shawn. *The Happiness Advantage: How a Positive Brain Fuels Success In Work and Life.* New York: Currency, 2018.

Aguilar, Elena. *The Art of Coaching: Effective Strategies for School Transformation.* San Francisco: Jossey-Bass, 2013.

Arriaga, Trudy Tuttle, Stacie Lynn Stanley, and Delores B. Lindsey. *Leading While Female: A Culturally Proficient Response for Gender Equity.* Thousand Oaks, CA: Corwin Press, 2020.

Banaji, Mahzarin R., & Anthony G. Greenwald. *Blindspot: Hidden Biases of Good People.* New York: Bantam Books, 2016.

Bloom, Gary, Claire Castagna, Ellen Moir, and Betsy Warren. *Blended Coaching: Skills and Strategies to Support Principal Development.* Thousand Oaks, CA: Corwin Press, 2005.

Brackett, Marc. *Permission to Feel: The Power of Emotional Intelligence to Achieve Well-Being and Success.* New York: Celadon Books, 2019.

Brown, Brené. *Braving the Wilderness: The Quest for True Belonging and the Courage to Stand Alone.* New York: Random House, 2017.

Brown, Brené. *Dare to Lead: Brave Work, Tough Conversations, Whole Hearts.* New York: Random House, 2018.

Brown, Brené. *The Gifts of Imperfection: Let Go of Who You Think You're Supposed to Be and Embrace Who You Are.* Center City, MN: Hazelden, 2010.

Burgess, Shelley, and Beth Houf. *Lead Like a Pirate: Make School Amazing for Your Students and Staff.* San Diego, CA: Dave Burgess Consulting, Inc., 2017.

Cabeen, Jessica. *Lead with Grace: Leaning into the Soft Skills of Leadership.* Highland Heights, OH: Times 10 Publications, 2019.

Cabeen, Jessica, Jessica Johnson, Sarah Johnson. *Balance Like a Pirate: Going beyond Work-Life Balance to Ignite Passion and Thrive as an Educator.* San Diego, CA: Dave Burgess Consulting, Inc., 2018.

Cliatt-Wayman, Linda. *Lead Fearlessly, Love Hard: Finding Your Purpose and Putting It to Work.* San Francisco: Jossey-Bass, 2017.

Cloud, Henry. *Necessary Endings: The Employees, Businesses, and Relationships That All of Us Have to Give Up in Order to Move Forward.* New York: Harper Collins, 2010.

Dweck, Carol S. *Mindset; The New Psychology of Success.* New York: Ballantine Books, 2008.

Eagly, Alice. H., and Linda L. Carli. "Women and the Labyrinth of Leadership." *Harvard Business Review*, September 2007. https://hbr.org/2007/09/women-and-the-labyrinth-of-leadership.

Fosslien, Liz, and Mollie West Duffy. *No Hard Feelings: The Secret Power of Embracing Emotions at Work.* New York: Portfolio/Penguin, 2019.

Gates, Melinda. *The Moment of Lift: How Empowering Women Changes the World.* New York: Flatiron Books, 2019.

Goldsmith, Marshall. *What Got You Here Won't Get You There: How Successful People Become Even More Successful!* With Mark Reiter. New York: Hyperion, 2007.

Goleman, Daniel. *Emotional Intelligence: Why It Can Matter More Than IQ.* New York: Bantam Books, 1995.

Grant, Adam. *Originals: How Non-Conformists Move the World.* New York: Penguin Books, 2016.

Hansen, Morten T. *Great at Work: How Top Performers Do Less, Work Better, and Achieve More.* New York: Simon & Schuster, 2018.

Helgesen, Sally, and Marshall Goldsmith. *How Women Rise: Break the 12 Habits Holding You Back.* London: Penguin Random House UK, 2018.

Hollis, Dave. *Get Out of Your Own Way: A Skeptic's Guide to Growth and Fulfillment.* New York: HarperCollins Leadership, 2020.

Hollis, Rachel. *Girl, Wash Your Face: Stop Believing the Lies About Who You Are So You Can Become Who You Were Meant to Be.* Nashville, TN: Nelson Books, 2018.

Hollis, Rachel. *Girl, Stop Apologizing: A Shame-Free Plan for Embracing and Achieving Your Goals.* Nashville, TN: Nelson Books, 2019.

Kay, Katty, and Claire Shipman. *The Confidence Code: The Science and Art of Self-Assurance—What Women Should Know.* New York: Harper Business, 2014.

Kiner, Mikaela. "It's Time to Break the Cycle of Female Rivalry." *Harvard Business Review,* April 14, 2020. https://hbr.org/2020/04/its-time-to-break-the-cycle-of-female-rivalry. Retrieved April 25, 2021.

Kise, Jane A. G., and Barbara K. Watterston. *Step In, Step Up: Empowering Women for the School Leadership Journey.* Bloomington, IN: Solution Tree, 2019.

Frankel, Lois P. *Nice Girls Don't Get the Corner Office: 101 Unconscious Mistakes Women Make That Sabotage Their Careers.* Warner Business Books, 2004.

Mack, Gary. *Mind Gym: An Athlete's Guide to Inner Excellence.* With David Casstevens. New York: McGraw-Hill, 2001.

Martineau, Jennifer W., and Portia R. Mount. *Kick Some Glass: 10 Ways Women Succeed at Work on Their Own Terms.* New York: McGraw-Hill Education, 2018.

Medcalf, Joshua. *Pound the Stone: 7 Lessons to Develop Grit on the Path to Mastery.* Self-published, Joshua Medcalf. (2017)

Mohr, Tara Sophia. "Why Women Don't Apply for Jobs Unless They're 100% Qualified." *Harvard Business Review,* August 25, 2014. https://hbr.org/2014/08/why-women-dont-apply-for-jobs-unless-theyre-100-qualified. Retrieved July 13, 2020.

Niequist, Shauna. *Present Over Perfect: Leaving Behind Frantic for a Simpler, More Soulful Way of Living.* Grand Rapids, MI: Zondervan, 2016.

Robbins, Mel. *The 5 Second Rule: Transform Your Life, Work, and Confidence with Everyday Courage.* Houston, TX: Savio Republic, 2017.

Sampson, Pauline M., Gloria Gresham, Stephanie Applewhite, and Kerry Roberts. "Women Superintendents: Promotion of Other Women to Central Office Administration." *Advancing Women in Leadership Journal* 35, (2015): 187–192. https://awl-ojs-tamu.tdl.org/awl/index.php/awl/article/view/139.

Sandberg, Sheryl. *Lean In: Women, Work, and the Will to Lead.* With Nell Scovell. New York: Alfred A. Knopf, 2013.

Saujani, Reshma. *Brave, Not Perfect: Fear Less, Fail More, and Live Bolder.* New York: Currency, 2019.

Schank, Hana, and Elizabeth Wallace. *The Ambition Decisions: What Women Know About Work, Family, and the Path to Building a Life.* New York: Viking, 2018.

Scott, Kim. *Radical Candor: Be a Kick-Ass Boss Without Losing Your Humanity.* New York: St. Martin's Press, 2019.

Stone, Douglas, and Sheila Heen. *Thanks for the Feedback: The Science and Art of Receiving Feedback Well (Even When It Is Off Base, Unfair, Poorly Delivered, and, Frankly, You're Not in the Mood).* New York: Penguin Books, 2015.

Acknowledgments

To our professional organization, the Coalition of Oregon School Administrators, we appreciate the support you have provided us in our leadership growth. Without the opportunities and encouragement you provide to administrators, we would have never met or grown into the leaders we are today.

To Dave Burgess Consulting, Inc and staff, your ongoing feedback and guidance was greatly appreciated. Thank you for believing in us.

To Shelley Burgess and Beth Houf, thank you for your encouragement and support to make the idea for this book a reality.

To all of the women contributors, thank you for taking the time to share your stories with us and with our readers.

To our husbands, thank you for supporting and listening to us, being our champions, and letting us talk way too fast for way too long. We are blessed to have you by our sides.

About the Authors

Dr. Rachael George

From fighting wildland fires with the US Forest Service to putting out fires in the classroom, education was the last place Rachael thought she'd end up. It wasn't until a hard conversation with a base manager in Grangeville, Idaho, that Rachael realized she needed to put her chainsaw down and make a bigger impact on the world. Rachael is a member of the ASCD Emerging Leaders Class of 2015 and currently serves as the executive director of student services and elementary programs in the Oregon Trail School District. She is the past principal of Sandy Grade School, and during her seven years there, they went from being one of the lowest-ranked elementary schools in the state of Oregon to performing in the top 20 percent. Sandy Grade School has been recognized by the International Center for Leadership in Education (ICLE) as a Model School for closing the achievement gap. Prior to serving as an elementary principal, she was a middle school principal of an "outstanding" and two-time "Level 5: Model School," as recognized by the state of Oregon. Rachael specializes in curriculum development and instructional improvement, as well as working with at-risk students and closing the achievement gap. She is also the coauthor of *PrincipalED: Navigating the Leadership Learning Curve.* Connect with Rachael on Twitter @DrRachaelGeorge.

Majalise Tolan

Majalise Tolan has been an energetic and proactive educator for eighteen years. She began her administrative career as a high school assistant principal and athletic director and has since served as an intermediate principal and high school principal. Before becoming secondary director of the Lincoln County School District in Oregon, she was the secondary teaching and learning administrator, overseeing curriculum and instruction, AVID (Advancement via Individual Determination), athletics, career and technical education, and the Title VI Bureau of Indian Education Program. Throughout her time working as a consultant, she has led multiple districts through standards, instruction, and assessment alignment work. She served as the 2020–2021 president for the Oregon Association of Secondary School Administrators and is actively involved in advocating for student voice. Connect with Majalise on Twitter @MajaliseTolan.

More from

Since 2012, DBCI has published books that inspire and equip educators to be their best. For more information on our titles or to purchase bulk orders for your school, district, or book study, visit DaveBurgessConsulting.com/DBCIbooks.

MORE FROM THE *LEAD LIKE A PIRATE*™ SERIES

Lead Like a PIRATE by Shelley Burgess and Beth Houf
Balance Like a PIRATE by Jessica Cabeen, Jessica Johnson, and Sarah Johnson
Lead beyond Your Title by Nili Bartley
Lead with Appreciation by Amber Teamann and Melinda Miller
Lead with Culture by Jay Billy
Lead with Instructional Rounds by Vicki Wilson
Lead with Literacy by Mandy Ellis

LIKE A PIRATE™ SERIES

Teach Like a PIRATE by Dave Burgess
eXPlore Like a PIRATE by Michael Matera
Learn Like a PIRATE by Paul Solarz
Plan Like a PIRATE by Dawn M. Harris
Play Like a PIRATE by Quinn Rollins
Run Like a PIRATE by Adam Welcome
Tech Like a PIRATE by Matt Miller

LEADERSHIP & SCHOOL CULTURE

Beyond the Surface of Restorative Practices by Marisol Rerucha
Choosing to See by Pamela Seda and Kyndall Brown

Culturize by Jimmy Casas

Discipline Win by Andy Jacks

Escaping the School Leader's Dunk Tank by Rebecca Coda and Rick Jetter

Fight Song by Kim Bearden

From Teacher to Leader by Starr Sackstein

If the Dance Floor Is Empty, Change the Song by Joe Clark

The Innovator's Mindset by George Couros

It's OK to Say "They" by Christy Whittlesey

Kids Deserve It! by Todd Nesloney and Adam Welcome

Let Them Speak by Rebecca Coda and Rick Jetter

The Limitless School by Abe Hege and Adam Dovico

Live Your Excellence by Jimmy Casas

Next-Level Teaching by Jonathan Alsheimer

The Pepper Effect by Sean Gaillard

Principaled by Kate Barker, Kourtney Ferrua, and Rachael George

The Principled Principal by Jeffrey Zoul and Anthony McConnell

Relentless by Hamish Brewer

The Secret Solution by Todd Whitaker, Sam Miller, and Ryan Donlan

Start. Right. Now. by Todd Whitaker, Jeffrey Zoul, and Jimmy Casas

Stop. Right. Now. by Jimmy Casas and Jeffrey Zoul

Teachers Deserve It by Rae Hughart and Adam Welcome

Teach Your Class Off by CJ Reynolds

They Call Me "Mr. De" by Frank DeAngelis

Thrive through the Five by Jill M. Siler

Unmapped Potential by Julie Hasson and Missy Lennard

When Kids Lead by Todd Nesloney and Adam Dovico

Word Shift by Joy Kirr

Your School Rocks by Ryan McLane and Eric Lowe

TECHNOLOGY & TOOLS

50 Things to Go Further with Google Classroom by Alice Keeler and Libbi Miller

50 Things You Can Do with Google Classroom by Alice Keeler and Libbi Miller

140 Twitter Tips for Educators by Brad Currie, Billy Krakower, and Scott Rocco

Block Breaker by Brian Aspinall

Building Blocks for Tiny Techies by Jamila "Mia" Leonard

Code Breaker by Brian Aspinall

The Complete EdTech Coach by Katherine Goyette and Adam Juarez

Control Alt Achieve by Eric Curts

The Esports Education Playbook by Chris Aviles, Steve Isaacs, Christine Lion-Bailey, and Jesse Lubinsky

Google Apps for Littles by Christine Pinto and Alice Keeler

Master the Media by Julie Smith

Raising Digital Leaders by Jennifer Casa-Todd

Reality Bytes by Christine Lion-Bailey, Jesse Lubinsky, and Micah Shippee, PhD

Sail the 7 Cs with Microsoft Education by Becky Keene and Kathi Kersznowski

Shake Up Learning by Kasey Bell

Social LEADia by Jennifer Casa-Todd

Stepping Up to Google Classroom by Alice Keeler and Kimberly Mattina

Teaching Math with Google Apps by Alice Keeler and Diana Herrington

Teachingland by Amanda Fox and Mary Ellen Weeks

Teaching with Google Jamboard by Alice Keeler and Kimberly Mattina

TEACHING METHODS & MATERIALS

All 4s and 5s by Andrew Sharos

Boredom Busters by Katie Powell

The Classroom Chef by John Stevens and Matt Vaudrey

The Collaborative Classroom by Trevor Muir

Copyrighteous by Diana Gill

CREATE by Bethany J. Petty

Ditch That Homework by Matt Miller and Alice Keeler

Ditch That Textbook by Matt Miller

Don't Ditch That Tech by Matt Miller, Nate Ridgway, and Angelia Ridgway

EDrenaline Rush by John Meehan
Educated by Design by Michael Cohen, The Tech Rabbi
The EduProtocol Field Guide by Marlena Hebern and Jon Corippo
The EduProtocol Field Guide: Book 2 by Marlena Hebern and Jon Corippo
The EduProtocol Field Guide: Math Edition by Lisa Nowakowski and Jeremiah Ruesch
Expedition Science by Becky Schnekser
Frustration Busters by Katie Powell
Fully Engaged by Michael Matera and John Meehan
Game On? Brain On! by Lindsay Portnoy, PhD
Guided Math AMPED by Reagan Tunstall
Innovating Play by Jessica LaBar-Twomy and Christine Pinto
Instant Relevance by Denis Sheeran
Keeping the Wonder by Jenna Copper, Ashley Bible, Abby Gross, and Staci Lamb
LAUNCH by John Spencer and A.J. Juliani
Make Learning MAGICAL by Tisha Richmond
Pass the Baton by Kathryn Finch and Theresa Hoover
Project-Based Learning Anywhere by Lori Elliott
Pure Genius by Don Wettrick
The Revolution by Darren Ellwein and Derek McCoy
Shift This! by Joy Kirr
Skyrocket Your Teacher Coaching by Michael Cary Sonbert
Spark Learning by Ramsey Musallam
Sparks in the Dark by Travis Crowder and Todd Nesloney
Table Talk Math by John Stevens
Unpack Your Impact by Naomi O'Brien and LaNesha Tabb
The Wild Card by Hope and Wade King
The Writing on the Classroom Wall by Steve Wyborney
You Are Poetry by Mike Johnston

INSPIRATION, PROFESSIONAL GROWTH & PERSONAL DEVELOPMENT

Be REAL by Tara Martin
Be the One for Kids by Ryan Sheehy

The Coach ADVenture by Amy Illingworth
Creatively Productive by Lisa Johnson
Educational Eye Exam by Alicia Ray
The EduNinja Mindset by Jennifer Burdis
Empower Our Girls by Lynmara Colón and Adam Welcome
Finding Lifelines by Andrew Grieve and Andrew Sharos
The Four O'Clock Faculty by Rich Czyz
How Much Water Do We Have? by Pete and Kris Nunweiler
P Is for Pirate by Dave and Shelley Burgess
A Passion for Kindness by Tamara Letter
The Path to Serendipity by Allyson Apsey
Sanctuaries by Dan Tricarico
Saving Sycamore by Molly B. Hudgens
The SECRET SAUCE by Rich Czyz
Shattering the Perfect Teacher Myth by Aaron Hogan
Stories from Webb by Todd Nesloney
Talk to Me by Kim Bearden
Teach Better by Chad Ostrowski, Tiffany Ott, Rae Hughart, and Jeff Gargas
Teach Me, Teacher by Jacob Chastain
Teach, Play, Learn! by Adam Peterson
The Teachers of Oz by Herbie Raad and Nathan Lang-Raad
TeamMakers by Laura Robb and Evan Robb
Through the Lens of Serendipity by Allyson Apsey
The Zen Teacher by Dan Tricarico

CHILDREN'S BOOKS

Beyond Us by Aaron Polansky
Cannonball In by Tara Martin
Dolphins in Trees by Aaron Polansky
I Can Achieve Anything by MoNique Waters
I Want to Be a Lot by Ashley Savage
The Princes of Serendip by Allyson Apsey
Ride with Emilio by Richard Nares
The Wild Card Kids by Hope and Wade King
Zom-Be a Design Thinker by Amanda